Stories of
Many
Cultures

Edited by
John Catron, Sue Hackman
and Jean Moore

Hodder Education
A MEMBER OF HACHETTE LIVRE UK

Acknowledgements can be found on page 131

Hachette's policy is to use papers that are natural, renewable and recyclable products and made from wood grown in sustainable forests. The logging and manufacturing processes are expected to conform to the environmental regulations of the country of origin.

Orders: please contact Bookpoint Ltd, 130 Milton Park, Abingdon, Oxon OX14 4SB. Telephone: (44) 01235 827720. Fax: (44) 01235 400454. Lines are open 9.00–5.00, Monday to Saturday, with a 24-hour message answering service. Visit our website at www.hoddereducation.co.uk

First published in 2008 by
Hodder Education,
part of Hachette Livre UK
338 Euston Road
London NW1 3BH

Impression number   10 9 8 7 6 5 4 3 2 1
Year   2013 2012 2011 2010 2009 2008

Cover photo © Images.com/Corbis
Typeset in 12/14 Bembo by Charon Tec Ltd (A Macmillan Company), Chennai, India www.charontec.com
Printed in Great Britain by CPI Antony Rowe.

A catalogue record for this title is available from the British Library

ISBN 978 0 340 96629 7

Contents

Frankie Mae

By Jean Wheeler Smith

The sun had just started coming up when the men gathered at the gate of the White Plantation. They leaned on the fence, waiting. No one was nervous, though. They'd all been waiting a long time. A few more minutes couldn't make much difference. They surveyed the land that they were leaving, the land from which they had brought forth seas of cotton.

Old Man Brown twisted around so that he leaned sideways on the gate. Even though he was in his fifties, he was still a handsome man. Medium-sized, with reddish-brown skin. His beard set him apart from the others; it was the same mixture of black and grey as his hair, but while his hair looked like wool, the strands of his beard were long and nearly straight. He was proud of it, and even when he wasn't able to take a bath, he kept his beard neatly cut and shaped into a V.

He closed his eyes. The sun was getting too bright; it made his headache worse. 'Damn,' he thought, 'I sure wouldn't be out here this early on no Monday morning if it wasn't for what we got to do today. Whisky'll sure kill you if you don't get some sleep long with it. I wasn't never just crazy 'bout doing this, anyway. Wonder what made me decide to go along?'

Then he smiled to himself. ''Course. It was on account a Frankie Mae. She always getting me into something.'

Frankie was his first child, born twenty-two years ago, during the war. When she was little, she had gone

1

everywhere with him. He had a blue bicycle with a rusty wire basket in the front. He used to put Frankie Mae in the basket and ride her to town with him and to the café, and sometimes they'd go nowhere special, just riding. She'd sit sideways so that she could see what was on the road ahead and talk with him at the same time. She never bothered to hold onto the basket; she knew her daddy wouldn't let her fall. Frankie fitted so well into the basket that for a few years the Old Man thought that it was growing with her.

She was a black child, with huge green eyes that seemed to glow in the dark. From the age of four on she had a look of being full-grown. The look was in her muscular, well-defined limbs that seemed like they could do a woman's work and in her way of seeing everything around her. Most times she was alive and happy. The only thing wrong with her was that she got hurt so easy. The slightest rebuke sent her crying; the least hint of disapproval left her moody and depressed for hours. But on the other side of it was that she had a way of springing back from pain. No matter how hurt she had been, she would be her old self by the next day. The Old Man worried over her. He wanted most to cushion her life.

When Frankie reached six, she became too large to ride in the basket with him. Also he had four more children by then. So he bought a car for forty dollars. Not long afterwards he became restless. He'd heard about how you could make a lot of money over in the delta. So he decided to go over there. He packed what he could carry in one load – the children, a few chickens, and a mattress – and slipped off one night.

Two days after they left the hills, they drove up to the White Plantation in Loflore County, Mississippi. They were given a two-room house that leaned to one side and five dollars to make some groceries with for the next month.

The Old Man and his wife, Mattie, worked hard that year. Up at four-thirty and out to the field. Frankie Mae stayed behind to nurse the other children and to watch the pot that was cooking for dinner. At sundown they came back home and got ready for the next day. They did a little sweeping, snapped some beans for dinner the next day, and washed for the baby. Then they sat on the porch together for maybe a half hour.

That was the time the Old Man liked best, the half hour before bed. He and Frankie talked about what had happened during the day, and he assured her that she had done a good job keeping up the house. Then he went on about how smart she was going to be when she started school. It would be in two years, when the oldest boy was big enough to take care of the others.

One evening on the porch Frankie said, 'A man from town come by today looking for our stove. You know the short one, the one ain't got no hair. Said we was three weeks behind and he was gonna take it. Had a truck to take it back in, too.'

The Old Man lowered his head. He was ashamed that Frankie had had to face that man by herself. No telling what he said to her. And she took everything so serious. He'd have to start teaching her how to deal with folks like that.

'What did you tell him, baby?' he asked. 'He didn't hurt you none, did he?'

'No, he didn't bother me, sides looking mean. I told him I just this morning seen some money come in the mail from Uncle Ed in Chicago. And I heard my daddy say he was gonna use it to pay off the stoveman. So he said "Well, I give y'all one more week, one more." And he left.'

The Old Man pulled Frankie to him and hugged her. 'You did 'zactly right, honey.' She understood. She would be able to take care of herself.

The end of the first year in the delta the Old Man and Mattie went to settle up. It was just before Christmas. When their turn came, they were called by Mr White Junior, a short fat man, with a big stomach, whose clothes were always too tight.

'Let me see, Johnnie,' he said. 'Here it is. You owe two hundred dollars.'

The Old Man was surprised. Sounded just like he was back in the hills. He had expected things to be different over here. He had made a good crop. Should have cleared something. Well, no sense in arguing. The bossman counted out fifty dollars.

'Here's you some Christmas money,' Mr White Junior said. 'Pay me when you settle up next year.'

The Old Man took the money to town that same day and bought himself some barrels and some pipes and a bag of chopped corn. He had made whisky in the hills, and he could make it over here, too. You could always find somebody to buy it. Wasn't no reason he should spend all his time farming if he couldn't make nothing out of it. He and Mattie put up their barrels in the trees down by the river and set their mash to ferment.

By spring Brown had a good business going. He sold to the coloured cafés and even to some of the white ones. And folks knew they could always come to his house if they ran out. He didn't keep the whisky at the house, though. Too dangerous, it was buried down by the water.

When folks came unexpected, it was up to Frankie and her brother next to her to go get the bottles. Nobody noticed children. The Old Man bought them a new red wagon for their job.

He was able to pay off his stove and give Mattie some money every once in a while. And they ate a little better now. But still they didn't have much more than before because Brown wasn't the kind of man to save. Also he had to do a lot of drinking himself to keep up his sales. Folks didn't like to drink by themselves. When he'd start to drinking, he usually spent up or gave away whatever he had in his pocket. So they still had to work as hard as ever for Mr White Junior. Brown enjoyed selling the whisky, though, and Mattie could always go out and sell a few bottles in case of some emergency like their lights being cut off. So they kept the business going.

That spring Mr White Junior decided to take them off shares. He would pay one dollar fifty a day for chopping cotton, and he'd pay by the hundred pound for picking. The hands had no choice. They could work by the day or leave. Actually, the Old Man liked it better working by the day. Then he would have more time to see to his whisky.

Also, Mr White Junior made Brown the timekeeper over the other hands. Everybody had drunk liquor with him, and most folks liked him. He could probably keep them working better than anybody else. He did fight too much. But the hands knew that he always carried his pistol. If anybody fought him, they'd have to be trying to kill him, 'cause he'd be trying to kill them.

Brown was given a large, battered watch. So he'd know what time to stop for dinner. His job was to see that the hands made a full day in the field and that all the weeds got chopped. The job was easier than getting out there chopping in all that sun. So Brown liked it. The only hard part was in keeping after the women whose time was about to come. He hated to see them dragging to the field, their bellies about to burst. They were supposed to keep up with the others, which was impossible. Oftentimes Mr White Junior slipped up on the work crew and found one of the big-bellied women lagging behind the others.

'Goddamit, Johnnie,' he'd say, 'I done told you to keep the hands together. Queenester is way behind. I don't pay good money for folks to be standing around. If she sick, she need to go home.'

Sometimes the Old Man felt like defending the woman. She had done the best she could. But then he'd think, No, better leave things like they is.

'You sure right, Mr White Junior. I was just 'bout to send her home myself. Some niggers too lazy to live.'

He would walk slowly across the field to the woman. 'I'm sorry, Queenester. The bossman done seen you. I told you all to be looking out for him! Now you got to go. You come back tomorrow, though. He won't hardly be back in this field so soon. I try and let you make two more days this week. I know you needs the little change.'

The woman would take up her hoe and start walking home. Mr White Junior didn't carry no hands except to eat dinner and to go home after the day had been made.

One day when he had carried the hands in from the field, Mr White Junior stopped the Old Man as he was climbing down from the back of the pick-up truck. While the bossman talked, Brown fingered his timekeeper's watch that hung on a chain from his belt.

6

'Johnnie,' Mr White Junior said, 'It don't look right to me for you to leave a girl at home that could be working when I need all the hands I can get. And you the time-keeper, too. This cotton can't wait on you all to get ready to chop it. I want Frankie Mae out there tomorrow.'

He had tried to resist. 'But we getting along with what me and Mattie makes. Ain't got nothing, but we eating. I wants Frankie Mae to go to school. We can do without the few dollars she would make.'

'I want my cotton chopped,' White said, swinging his fat sweating body into the truck. 'Get that girl down here tomorrow. Don't nobody stay in my house and don't work.'

That night the Old Man dreaded the half hour on the porch. When Frankie had started school that year, she had already been two years late. And she had been so excited about going.

When the wood had been gathered and the children cleaned up, he followed Frankie onto the sloping porch. She fell to telling him about the magnificent yellow bus in which she rode to school. He sat down next to her on the step.

'Frankie Mae, I'm going to tell you something.'

'What's that, Daddy? Mamma say I been slow 'bout helping 'round the house since I been going to school? I do better. Guess I lost my head.'

'No, baby. That ain't it at all. You been helping your Mama fine.' He stood up to face her but could not bring his eyes to the level of her bright, happy face.

'Mr White Junior stopped me today when I was getting off the truck. Say he want you to come to field till the chopping get done.'

She found his eyes. 'What did you say, Daddy?'

'Well, I told him you wanted to go to school, and we could do without your little money. But he say you got to go.'

The child's eyes lost their brilliance. Her shoulders slumped, and she began to cry softly. Tired, the Old Man sat back down on the step. He took her hand and sat with her until long after Mattie and the other children had gone to bed.

The next morning Frankie was up first. She put on two blouses and a dress and some pants to keep off the sun and found herself a rag to tie around her head. Then she woke up her daddy and the others, scolding them for being so slow.

'We got to go get all that cotton chopped! And y'all laying round wasting good daylight. Come on.'

Brown got up and threw some water on his face. He saw Frankie bustling around in her layers of clothes, looking like a little old woman, and he smiled. That's how Frankie Mae was. She'd feel real bad, terrible for a few hours, but she always snapped back. She'd be all right now.

On the way to the field he said, 'Baby, I'm gonna make you the water girl. All you got to do is carry water over to them that hollers for it and keep your bucket full. You don't have to chop none lest you see Mr White Junior coming.'

'No, Daddy, that's all right. The other hands'll say you was letting me off easy 'cause I'm yours. Say you taking advantage of being timekeeper. I go on and chop with the rest.'

He tried to argue with her, but she wouldn't let him give her the water bucket. Finally he put her next to Mattie so she could learn from her. As he watched over the field, he set himself not to think about his child inhaling the cotton dust and insecticide. When his eyes happened on her and Mattie, their backs bent way over, he quickly averted them. Once, when he jerked his eyes away, he found instead the bright yellow school bus bouncing along the road.

Frankie learned quickly how to chop the cotton, and sometimes she even seemed to enjoy herself. Often the choppers would go to the store to buy sardines and crackers and beans for their dinner instead of going home. At the store the Old Man would eat his beans from their jagged-edge can and watch with pride as Frankie laughed and talked with everyone and made dates with the ladies to attend church on the different plantations. Every Sunday Frankie had a service to go to. Sometimes, when his head wasn't bad from drinking, the Old Man went with her because he liked so much to see her enjoy herself. Those times he put a few gallons of his whisky in the back of the car just in case somebody needed them. When he and Frankie went off to church like that, they didn't usually get back till late at night. They would be done sold all the whisky and the Old Man would be talking loud about the wonderful sermon that the reverend had preached and all the souls that had come to Jesus.

That year they finished the chopping in June. It was too late to send Frankie back to school, and she couldn't go again until after the cotton had been picked. When she went back in November she had missed four months and found it hard to keep up with the children who'd been going all the time. Still, she went every day that she could. She stayed home only when she had to, when her mother was sick or when, in the cold weather, she didn't have shoes to wear.

Whenever she learned that she couldn't go to school on a particular day, she withdrew into herself for about an hour. She had a chair near the stove, where she sat, and the little children knew not to bother her. After the hour she'd push back her chair and go to stirring the cotton in the bed ticks or washing the greens for dinner.

If this was possible, the Old Man loved her still more now. He saw the children of the other workers and his own children, too, get discouraged and stop going to school. They said it was too confusing; they never knew what the teacher was talking about because they'd not been there the day before or the month before. And they resented being left behind in classes with children half their size. He saw the other children get so that they wouldn't hold themselves up, wouldn't try to be clean and make folks respect them. Yet every other day Frankie managed to put on a clean starched dress, and she kept at her lessons.

By the time Frankie was thirteen she could figure as well as the preacher, and she was made secretary of the church.

That same year she asked her daddy if she could keep a record of what they made and what they spent.

'Sure, baby,' he said. 'I'll be proud for you to do it. We might even come out a little better this year when we settle up. I tell you what. If we get some money outta Mr White Junior this year, I'll buy you a dress for Christmas, a red one.'

Frankie bought a black-and-white-speckled note-book. She put in it what they made and what they paid on their bill. After chopping time she became excited. She figured they had just about paid the bill out. What they made from picking should be theirs. She and the Old Man would sit on the porch and go over the figures and plan for Christmas. Sometimes they even talked about taking a drive up to Chicago to see Uncle Ed. Every so often he would try to hold down her excitement by reminding her that their figures had to be checked against the bossman's. Actually, he didn't expect to do much better than he'd done all the other years. But she was so proud to be using what she had learned, her numbers and all. He hated to discourage her.

Just before Christmas they went to settle up. When it came to the Old Man's turn, he trembled a little. He knew it was almost too much to hope for, that they would have money coming to them. But some of Frankie's excitement had rubbed off on him.

He motioned to her, and they went up to the table where there were several stacks of ten and twenty dollar bills, a big ledger, and a pistol. Mr White Junior sat in a brown chair, and his agent stood behind him. Brown took heart from the absolute confidence with which Frankie Mae walked next to him, and he controlled his trembling. Maybe the child was right and they had something coming to them.

'Hey there, Johnnie,' Mr White Junior said, 'see you brought Frankie Mae along. Fine, fine. Good to start them early. Here's you a seat.'

The Old Man gave Frankie the one chair and stood beside her. The bossman rifled his papers and came out with a long narrow sheet. Brown recognized his name at the top.

'Here you are, Johnnie, y'all come out pretty good this year. Proud of you. Don't owe but $65. Since you done so good, gonna let you have $100 for Christmas.'

Frankie Mae spoke up. 'I been keeping a book for my daddy. And I got some different figures. Let me show you.'

The room was still. Everyone, while pretending not to notice the girl, was listening intently to what she said.

Mr White Junior looked surprised, but he recovered quickly.

'Why sure. Be glad to look at your figures. You know it's easy to make a mistake. I'll show you what you done wrong.'

Brown clutched her shoulder to stop her from handing over the book. But it was too late. Already she was leaning over the table, comparing her figures with those in the ledger.

'See, Mr White Junior, when we was chopping last year we made $576, and you took $320 of that to put on our bill. There. There it is on your book. And we borrowed $35 in July. There it is . . .'

The man behind the table grew red. One of his fat hands gripped the table while the other moved toward the pistol.

Frankie Mae finished. 'So you see, you owe us $180 for the year.'

The bossman stood up to gain the advantage of his height. He seemed about to burst. His eyes flashed around the room, and his hand clutched the pistol. He was just raising it from the table when he caught hold of himself. He took a deep breath and let go of the gun.

'Oh, yeah. I remember what happened now, Johnnie. It was that slip I gave to the doctor for Willie B. You remember, last year, 'fore chopping time. I got the bill last week. Ain't had time to put it in my book. It came to, let me think. Yeah, that was $350.'

The Old Man's tension fell away from him, and he resumed his normal manner. He knew exactly what the bossman was saying. It was as he had expected, as it had always been.

'Let's go, baby,' he said.

But Frankie didn't get up from the chair. For a moment she looked puzzled. Then her face cleared. She said, 'Willie didn't have anything wrong with him but a broken arm. The doctor spent twenty minutes with him one time and ten minutes the other. That couldn't cost no $350!'

The bossman's hand found the pistol again and gripped it until the knuckles were white. Brown pulled Frankie to him and put his arm around her. With his free hand he fingered his own pistol, which he always carried in his pocket. He was not afraid. But he hated the thought of shooting the man; even if he just nicked him, it would be the end for himself. He drew a line: If Mr White Junior touched him or Frankie, he would shoot. Short of that he would leave without a fight.

White spat thick, brown tobacco juice onto the floor, spattering it on the Old Man and the girl. 'Nigger,' he said, 'I know you ain't disputing my word. Don't nobody live on my place and call me no liar. That bill was $350. You understand me?' He stood tense, staring with hatred at the man and the girl. Everyone waited for Brown's answer. The Old Man felt Frankie's arms go 'round his waist.

'Tell him no, Daddy. We right, not him. I kept them figures all year, they got to be right.' The gates of the state farm flashed through the Old Man's mind. He thought of Mattie, already sick from high blood, trying to make a living for eleven people. Frankie's arms tightened.

'Yessir,' he said. 'I understand.'

The girl's arms dropped from him, and she started to the door. The other workers turned away to fiddle with a piece of rope, to scold a child. Brown accepted the $50 that was thrown across the table to him. As he turned to follow Frankie, he heard Mr White Junior's voice, low now and with a controlled violence. 'Hey you, girl. You, Frankie Mae.' She stopped at the door but didn't turn around.

'Long as you live, bitch, I'm gonna be right and you gonna be wrong. Now get your black ass outta here.'

Frankie stumbled out to the car and crawled onto the back seat. She cried all the way home. Brown tried to quiet her. She could still have the red dress. They'd go down to the river tomorrow and start on a new batch of whisky.

The next morning he laid in bed waiting to hear Frankie Mae moving around and fussing, waiting to know that she had snapped back to her old self. He laid there until everyone in the house had gotten up. Still he did not hear her. Finally he got up and went over to where she was balled up in the quilts.

He woke her. 'Come on, baby. Time to get up. School bus be here soon.'

'I ain't goin' today,' she said, 'got a stomach ache.'

Brown sat out on the porch all day long, wishing that she would get up out the bed and struggling to under-stand what had happened. This time Frankie had not bounced back to her old bright-eyed self. The line that held her to this self had been stretched too taut. It had lost its tension and couldn't pull her back.

Frankie never again kept a book for her daddy. She lost interest in things such as numbers and reading. She went to school as an escape from chores but got so little of her lessons done that she was never promoted from the fourth grade to the fifth. When she was fifteen and in the fourth grade, she had her first child. After that there was no more thought of school. In the following four years she had three more children.

She sat around the house, eating and growing fat. When well enough, she went to the field with her daddy. Her dresses were seldom ironed now. Whatever she could find to wear would do.

Still there were a few times, maybe once every three or four months, when she was lively and fresh. She'd get dressed and clean the children up and have her daddy drive them to church. On such days she'd be the first one up. She would have food on the stove before anybody else had a chance to dress. Brown would load up his trunk with whisky, and they'd stay all day.

It was for these isolated times that the Old Man waited. They kept him believing that she would get to be all right. Until she died, he woke up every morning listening for her laughter, waiting for her to pull the covers from his feet and scold him for being lazy.

She died giving birth to her fifth child. The midwife, Esther, was good enough, but she didn't know what to do when there were complications. Brown couldn't get up but $60 of the $100 cash that you had to deposit at the county hospital. So they wouldn't let Frankie in. She bled to death on the hundred-mile drive to the charity hospital in Vicksburg.

The Old Man squinted up at the fully risen sun. The bossman was late. Should have been at the gate by now. Well, it didn't matter. Just a few more minutes and they'd be through with the place forever.

His thoughts went back to the time when the civil rights workers had first come around and they had started their meetings up at the store. They'd talked about voting and about how plantation workers should be making enough to live off. Brown and the other men had listened and talked and agreed. So they decided to ask Mr White Junior for a raise. They wanted nine dollars for their twelve-hour day.

They had asked. And he had said, Hell no. Before he'd raise them he'd lower them. So they agreed to ask him again. And if he still said no, they would go on strike.

At first Brown hadn't understood himself why he agreed to the strike. It was only this morning that he realised why: It wasn't the wages or the house that was falling down 'round him and Mattie. It was that time when he went to ask Mr White Junior about the other $40 that he needed to put Frankie in the hospital.

'Sorry, Johnnieboy,' he'd said, patting Brown on the back, 'but me and Miz White having a garden party today and I'm so busy. You know how women are. She want me there every minute. See me tomorrow. I'll fix you up then.'

A cloud of dust rose up in front of Brown. The boss-man was barrelling down the road in his pick-up truck. He was mad. That was what he did when he got mad, drove his truck up and down the road fast. Brown chuckled. When they got through with him this morning, he might run that truck into the river.

Mr White Junior climbed down from the truck and made his way over to the gate. He began to give the orders for the day, who would drive the tractors, what fields would be chopped. The twelve men moved away from the fence, disdaining any support for what they were about to do.

16

One of the younger ones, James Lee, spoke up. 'Mr White Junior, we wants to know is you gonna raise us like we asked?'

'No, goddammit. Now go on, do what I told you.'

'Then,' James Lee continued, 'we got to go on strike from this place.'

James Lee and the others left the gate and went to have a strategy meeting up at the store about what to do next.

The Old Man was a little behind the rest because he had something to give Mr White Junior. He went over the sweat-drenched, cursing figure and handed him the scarred timekeeper's watch, the watch that had ticked away Frankie Mae's youth in the hot, endless rows of cotton.

Coffee for the Road

By Alex la Guma

They were past the maize-lands and driving through the wide, low, semi-desert country that sprawled away on all sides in reddish brown flats and depressions. The land, going south, was scattered with shrub and thorn bushes, like a vast unswept carpet. Far to the right, the metal vanes of a windmill pump turned wearily in the faint morning breeze, as if it had just been wakened to set reluctantly about its duty of sucking water from the miserly earth. The car hurled along the asphalt road, its tyres roaring along the black surface.

'I want another sandwich, please,' Zaida said. She huddled in the blanketed space among the suitcases in the back. She was six years old and weary from the long, speeding journey, and her initial interest in the landscape had evaporated, so that now she sagged tiredly in the padded space, ignoring the parched gullies and stunted trees that whisked past.

'There's some in the tin. You can help yourself, can't you?' the woman at the wheel said, without taking her eyes off the road. 'Do you want to eat some more, too, Ray?'

'Not hungry any more,' the boy beside her replied. He was gazing out at the barbed-wire fence that streamed back outside the turned-up window.

'How far's it to Cape Town, Mummy?' Zaida asked, munching a sandwich.

'We'll be there tomorrow afternoon,' the woman said.

'Will Papa be waiting?'

'Of course.'

'There's some sheep,' the boy, Ray, said. A scattering of farm buildings went by, drab, domino-shaped structures along a brown slope.

The mother had been travelling all night and she was fatigued, her eyes red, with the feeling of sand under the lids, irritating the eyeballs. They had stopped for a short while along the road, the night before; parked in a gap off the road outside a small town. There had been nowhere to put up for the night: the hotels were for Whites only. In fact, only Whites lived in these towns and everybody else, except for the servants, lived in tumbledown mud houses in the locations beyond. Besides, they did not know anybody in this part of the country.

Dawn had brought depression, gloom, ill-temper, which she tried to control in the presence of her children. After having parked on that stretch of road until after midnight, she had started out again and driven, the children asleep, through the rest of the night.

Now she had a bad headache, too, and when Zaida said, 'Can I have a meatball, Mummy?' she snapped back irritably: 'Oh dash it all! It's there, eat it, can't you?'

The landscape ripped by, like a film being run backwards, red-brown, yellow-red, pink-red, all studded with sparse bushes and broken boulders. To the east a huge outcrop of rock strata rose abruptly from the arid earth, like a titanic wedge of purple-lavender-layered cake topped with chocolate-coloured boulders. The car passed over a stretch of gravel road and the red dust boiled behind it like a flame-shot smoke-screen. A bird, its long, ribbon-like tail streaming behind it, skimmed the brush beyond the edge of the road, flitting along as fast as the car.

'Look at that funny bird, Mummy,' the boy, Ray, cried, and pressed his face to the dust-filmed glass.

The mother ignored him, trying to relax behind the wheel, her feet moving unconsciously, but skilfully, on the pedals in the floor. She thought that it would have been better to have taken a train, but Billy had written that he'd need the car because he had a lot of contacts to visit. She hoped the business would be better in the Cape. Her head ached, and she drove automatically. She was determined to finish the journey as quickly as possible.

Ray said, 'I want some coffee.' And he reached for the thermos flask on the rack under the dashboard. Ray could take care of himself, he did not need to have little things done for him.

'Give me some, too,' Zaida called from the back, among the suitcases.

'Don't be greedy,' Ray said to her. 'Eating, eating, eating.'

'I'm not greedy. I want a drink of coffee.'

'You had coffee this morning.'

'I want some more.'

'Greedy. Greedy.'

'Children,' the mother said wearily, 'children, stop that arguing.'

'He started first,' Zaida said.

'Stop it. Stop it,' the mother told her.

Ray was unscrewing the cap of the thermos. When it was off he drew the cork and looked in. 'Man, there isn't any,' he said. 'There isn't any more coffee.'

'Well, that's just too bad,' the mother said.

'I want a drink,' Zaida cried. 'I'm thirsty, I want some coffee.'

The mother smiled wearily: 'Oh, all right. But you've got to wait. We'll get some somewhere up the road. But wait, will you?'

The sun was a coppery smear in the flat blue sky, and the countryside, scorched yellow and brown, like an immense slice of toast, quivered and danced in the haze. The woman drove on, tiredly, her whole mind rattling like a stale nut. Behind the sunglasses her eyes were red-rimmed and there was a stretched look about the dark, handsome, Indian face. Her whole system felt taut and stretched like the wires of a harp, but too tight so that a touch might snap any one of them.

The miles purred and growled and hummed past: flat country and dust-coloured *koppies*, the baked clay *dongas* and low ridges of hills. A shepherd's hut, lonely as a lost soul, crouched against the shale-covered side of a flat hill; now and then a car passed theirs headed in the opposite direction, going north, crashing by in a shrill whine of a slip-stream. The glare of the sun quivered and quaked as if the air was boiling.

'I want some coffee,' Zaida repeated petulantly. 'We didn't have no coffee.'

'We'll buy some coffee,' her mother told her. 'We'll buy some for the road as soon as we get to a café. Stop it, now. Eat another sandwich.'

'Don't want sandwich. Want coffee.'

A group of crumbling huts, like scattered, broken cubes passed them in a hollow near the road and a band of naked, dusty brown children broke from the cover of a sheep-pen, dashing to the side of the road, cheering and waving at the car. Ray waved back, laughing, and then they were out of sight. The wind-scoured metal pylon of a water-pump drew up and then disappeared too.

21

Three black men trudged in single file along the roadside, looking ahead into some unknown future, wrapped in tattered, dusty blankets, oblivious of the heat, their heads shaded by the ruins of felt hats. They did not waver as the car spun past them but walked with fixed purpose.

The car slowed down for a steel-slung bridge and they rumbled over the dry, rock-strewn bed of a stream. A few sheep, their fleeces black with dust, sniffed among the boulders, watched by a man like a scarecrow.

At a distance, they passed the coloured location and then the African location, hovels of clay and clapboard strewn like discoloured dice along a brown slope, with tiny people and ant-like dogs moving among them. On another slope the name of the town was spelled out in whitewashed boulders.

The car passed the sheds of a railway siding, with the sheep milling in corrals, then lurched over the crossing and bounced back on to the roadway. A coloured man went by on a bicycle, and they drove slowly past the nondescript brown front of the Railway Hotel, a line of stores, and beyond a burnt hedge a group of white men with red, sun-skinned, wind-honed faces sat drinking at tables in front of another hotel with an imitation Dutch-colonial façade. There was other traffic parked along the dusty, gravel street of the little town: powdered cars and battered pick-up trucks, a wagon in front of a feed store. An old Coloured man swept the pavement in front of a shop, his reed broom making a hissing sound, like gas escaping in spurts.

Two white youths, pink-faced and yellow-haired, dressed in khaki shirts and shorts, stared at the car, their eyes suddenly hostile at the sight of a dark woman driving its shiny newness, metal fittings factory-smooth under the film of road dust. The car spun a little cloud behind it as it crept along the red-gravel street.

'What's the name of this place, Mummy?' the boy, Ray, asked. 'I don't know', the mother replied, tired, but glad to be able to slow down. 'Just some place in the Karroo.'

'What's the man doing?' Zaida asked, peering out through the window.

'Where?' Ray asked, looking about. 'What man?'

'He's gone now,' the little girl said. 'You didn't look quickly.' Then, 'Will we get some coffee now?'

'I think so,' the mother said. 'You two behave yourselves and there'll be coffee. Don't you want a cool drink?'

'No,' the boy said. 'You just get thirsty again, afterwards.'

'I want a lot of coffee with lots of sugar,' Zaida said.

'All right,' the mother said. 'Now stop talking such a lot.'

Up ahead, at the end of a vacant lot, stood a café. Tubular steel chair and tables stood on the pavement outside, in front of its shaded windows. Its front was decorated with old Coca Cola signs and painted menus. A striped awning shaded the tables. In the wall facing the vacant space was a foot-square hole where non-Whites were served, and a group of ragged Coloured and African people stood in the dust and tried to peer into it, their heads together, waiting with forced patience.

The mother drove the car up and brought it to a stop in front of the café. Inside a radio was playing and the slats of the venetian blinds in the windows were clean and dustless.

'Give me the flask,' the mother said, and took the thermos bottle from the boy. She unlatched the door. 'Now, you children, just sit quiet. I won't be long.'

She opened the door and slid out and, standing for a moment on the pavement, felt the exquisite relief of loosened muscles. She straightened body. But her head still ached badly and that spoiled the momentary delight which she felt. With the feeling gone, her brain was tired again and the body once more a tight-wound spring. She straightened the creases out of the smart tan suit she was wearing but left the jacket unbuttoned. Then, carrying the thermos flask, she crossed the sidewalk, moving between the plastic-and-steel furniture into the café.

Inside, the café was cool and lined with glass cases displaying cans and packages like specimens in some futuristic museum.

From somewhere at the back of the place came the smell and sound of potatoes being fried. An electric fan buzzed on a shelf and two gleaming urns, one of tea and the other of coffee, steamed against the back wall.

The only other customer was a small white boy with tow-coloured hair, a face like a near-ripe apple and a running nose. He wore a washed-out print shirt and khaki shorts, and his dusty bare feet were yellow-white and horny with cracked callouses. His pink, sticky mouth explored the surface of a lollipop while he scanned the row of outdated magazines in a wire rack.

Behind the glass counter and a trio of soda fountains a broad, heavy woman in a green smock thumbed through a stack of accounts, ignoring the group of dark faces pressing around the square hole in the side wall. She had a round-shouldered, thick body and reddish-complexioned face that looked as if it had been sand-blasted into its component parts: hard plains of cheeks and knobbly cheek-bones and a bony ridge of nose that separated twin pools of dull grey; and the mouth a bitter gash, cold and malevolent as a lizard's, a dry, chapped and serrated pink crack.

She looked up and started to say something, then saw the colour of the other woman and, for a moment, the grey pools of the eyes threatened to spill over as she gaped. The thin pink mouth writhed like a worm as she sought for words.

'Can you fill this flask with coffee for me, please?' the mother asked.

The crack opened and a screech came from it, harsh as the sound of metal rubbed against stone. 'Coffee? My Lord Jesus Christ!' the voice screeched. 'A bedamned *coolie* girl in here!' The eyes stared in horror at the brown, tired, handsome Indian face with its smart sunglasses, and the city cut of the tan suit. 'Coolies, Kaffirs and Hottentots outside,' she screamed. 'Don't you bloody well know? And you talk *English*, too, hey!'

The mother stared at her, startled, and then somewhere inside her something went off, snapped like a tight-wound spring suddenly loose, jangling shrilly into action, and she cried out with disgust as her arm came up and the thermos flask hurtled at the white woman.

'Bloody white trash!' she cried. 'Coolie yourself!'

The flask spun through the air and, before the woman behind the counter could ward it off, it struck her forehead above an eyebrow, bounced away, tinkling as the thin glass inside the metal cover shattered. The woman behind the counter screeched and clapped a hand to the bleeding gash over her eye, staggering back. The little boy dropped his lollipop with a yelp and dashed out. The dark faces at the square hatch gasped. The dark woman turned and stalked from the café in a rage.

25

She crossed the sidewalk, her brown face taut with anger and opened the door of her car furiously. The group of non-whites from the hole in the wall around the side of the building came to the edge of the vacant lot and stared at her as she slammed the door of the car and started the motor.

She drove savagely away from the place, her hands gripping the wheel tightly, so that the knuckles showed yellow through the brown skin. Then she recovered herself and relaxed wearily, slowing down, feeling tired again, through her anger. She took her time out of town while the children gazed, sensing that something was wrong.

Then the boy, Ray, asked, 'Isn't there any coffee, Mummy? And where's the flask?'

'No, there isn't any coffee,' the mother replied. 'We'll have to do without coffee, I'm afraid.'

'I wanted coffee,' the little girl, Zaida, complained.

'You be good,' the mother said. 'Mummy's tired. And please stop chattering.'

'Did you lose the flask?' Ray asked.

'Keep quiet, keep quiet,' the woman told him, and they lapsed into silence.

They drove past the edge of the town, past a dusty service station with its red pumps standing like sentinels before it. Past a man carrying a huge bundle of firewood on his head, and past the last buildings of the little town: a huddle of whitewashed cabins with chickens scrabbling in the dooryard, a sagging shearing-shed with a pile of dirty bales of wool inside, and a man hanging over a fence, watching them go by.

The road speared once more into the yellow-red-brown countryside and the last green trees dwindled away. The sun danced and jigged like a midday ghost across the expressionless earth, and the tyres of the car rumbled faintly on the black asphalt. There was some traffic ahead of them but the woman did not bother trying to overtake.

The boy broke the silence in the car by saying, 'Will Papa take us for drives?'

'He will, I know,' Zaida said. 'I like this car better than Uncle Ike's.'

'Well, *he* gave us lots of rides,' Ray replied. 'There goes one of those funny birds again.'

'Mummy, will we get some coffee later on?' Zaida asked.

'Maybe, dear. We'll see,' the mother said.

The dry and dusty landscape continued to flee past the window on either side of the car. Up ahead the sparse traffic on the road was slowing down and the mother eased her foot of the accelerator.

'Look at that hill,' the boy Ray, cried. 'It looks like a face.'

'Is it a real face?' Zaida asked, peering out.

'Don't be silly,' Ray answered. 'How can it be a real face? It just *looks* like a face.'

The car slowed down and the mother, thrusting her head through the window, peered forward past the car in front and saw the roadblock beyond it.

A small riot-van, a Land Rover, its windows and spotlight screened with thick wire mesh, had been pulled up half-way across the road, and a dusty automobile parked opposite to it, forming a barrier with just a car-wide space between them. A policeman in khaki shirt, trousers and flat cap leaned against the front fender of the automobile and held a Sten-gun across his thighs.

Another man in khaki sat at the wheel of the car, and a third policeman stood by the gap, directing the traffic through after examining the drivers.

The car ahead slowed down as it came up to the gap, the driver pulled up and the policeman looked at him, stepped back and waved him on. The car went through, revved and rolled away.

The policeman turned towards the next car, holding up a hand, and the mother driving the car felt the sudden pounding of her heart. She braked and waited, watching the khaki-clad figure strolling the short distance towards her.

He had a young face, with the usual red-burned complexion of the land, under the shiny leather bill of the cap. He was smiling thinly but the smile did not reach his eyes which bore the hard quality of chips of granite. He wore a holstered pistol at his waist, and, coming up, he turned towards the others and called, 'This looks like the one.'

The man with the Sten-gun straightened but did not come forward. His companion inside the car just looked across at the woman.

The policeman in the road said, still smiling slightly: 'Ah, we have been waiting for you. You didn't think they'd phone ahead, hey?'

The children in the car sat dead still, staring, their eyes troubled. The mother said, looking out: 'What's it all about?'

'Never mind what it's all about,' the policeman said to her. '*You* know what it's all about.' He looked her over and nodded. '*Ja*, darkie girl with brown suit and sunglasses. You're under arrest.'

'What's it all about?' the woman asked again. Her voice was not anxious, but she was worried about her children.

'Never mind. You'll find out,' the policeman told her coldly. 'One of those agitators making trouble here. Awright, listen.' He peered at her with flint-hard eyes. 'You turn the car around and don't try no funny business, hey? Our car will be in front and the van behind, so watch out.' His voice was cold and threatening.

'Where are you taking us? I've got to get my children to Cape Town.'

'I don't care about that,' he said. 'You make trouble here then you got to pay for it.' He looked back at the police car and waved a hand. The driver of the police car started it up and backed and then turned into the road.

'You follow that motor car,' the policeman said. 'We're going back that way.'

The woman said nothing but started her own car, manoeuvring it until they were behind the police car.

'Now don't you try any funny tricks,' the policeman said again. She stared at him and her eyes were also cold now. He went back to the riot-truck and climbed in. The car in front of her put on speed and she swung behind it, with the truck following.

'Where are we going, Mummy?' asked Zaida.

'You be quiet and behave yourselves,' the mother said, driving after the police car.

The countryside, red-brown and dusty, moved past them: the landscapes they had passed earlier now slipping the other way. The blue sky danced and wavered and the parched, scrub-strewn scenery stretched away around them in the yellow glare of the sun.

'I wish we had some coffee,' the little girl, Zaida, said.

Snowdrop

By Mei Chi Chan

She had come to tell them of her decision.

Standing by the door of the kitchen in the semi-darkness, a faint odour of bleach and onions greeted her like an old and comfortable companion. Silence, condensed by the hum of the refrigerators, echoed through and drew her in.

The florescent strips flickered before exploding off the hard, sharp surfaces, pricking out the edges, threatening the shadows. This was a kitchen that spoke not of home and its comforts but of forges, armoury and battle. For now, the steel rested. The oil in the deep fryer was cool, brown and thick as treacle. The heavy iron range stood dominating the room like an altar; the four holes cut side by side into its black metal looked curiously vulnerable to her, and she resisted the temptation to cover them up with the woks that huddled upside down like turtles beneath the range.

She walked across the room to the chopping board that stood on its own. Knives and choppers of different shapes and sizes hung from one of its edges, resembling a set of monstrous teeth. She could almost hear the thud of a heavy blade cleaving through flesh and bone onto the wood below. Delicately, she traced the scars on the surface. Tiny fragments of wood tickled her fingertips. In two hours her mother would come down the stairs and enter this arena. The fires would be lit, the oil would begin to bubble and steam and the steel would start to clash. She remembered Friday nights when she was a child. Friday was the busiest night of the week. People invaded the take-away in hordes after the pubs had closed. Reeking of cigarette smoke and with the sour smell of drink on their breath, they demanded to be fed. Inside the kitchen she would sit, unable to help: the still centre in the madly spinning wheel of movement around her. She would look backwards and forwards between her father and her mother. Their faces frightened her, she could not recognise them. They were not their daytime selves, they became something impersonal, mechanical, and even monstrous. They were like the knives, slashing, paring, chopping, slicing, dividing. Moving through the thick greasy white smoke like the warriors of old, advancing in the mists of dawn; they looked invincible. Every ounce of being was consumed in the task of making food. It could not be called 'cooking'. Cooking sounded too homely. No, like alchemists, they brought forth food out of steel and fire. Their creations subdued and sated the hungry hordes that bayed impatiently outside.

She walked over and bent down to pick up one of the steel woks beneath the range. She tested it for its weight, savouring the way it felt to grip the wooden handle in her hand and the tension stretching her wrist. She dropped it onto one of the holes and it made a dull clunk as it landed. She walked round and round the kitchen, circling the aluminum worktop that was the centrepiece of the room. At times, she would stride, eyes wide and blazing. Then at other times her steps turned into a shuffle. She sighed and muttered, shaking her head: *I can't, I can't do it, I can't, I really can't. They can. But not me. I'm too soft, too weak, too split. I don't have it — what it takes. I — will — fail.*

But there was another voice in her head, saying: *you can, you can do it. Of course you can. You have had the training. You have the guts. You have stamina. That's all you need. The rest will take care of itself.* She heard footsteps. She felt a shaking in the depths of her stomach. They would ask her and she would not know what to say . . .

★ ★ ★

'Snowdrop. That's a snowdrop.' The little girl listened deeply to the word. Gem-like, it sank into her heart and made it glow. A blue-green stem, a slender arch over virginal snow, and a white pendant flower dangling like an echo over it. 'A snowdrop.' That first, never-ending winter in England. Frosted air that bit her lungs, toes that never thawed, strangers made stranger still, wrapped and hunched and invisible in their layers, voices that blew like gusts into her ears, sound without meaning – until the word 'snowdrop'. Something melted. It was the feeling that she could not express then, the feeling of a fragile white flower rising over the snow. Now she would call it 'hope'. How thankful she was not to have known the word then.

They would ask her and she would say 'snowdrop' and they would understand. The word would turn like a key in their hearts. Snowdrop, snow-drop, a flower, a drop of . . .

Her mother and father broke into the space and light. She looked at them for a moment and there was confusion. In her mind they had been giants. Had they always been so small? How sallow and faded they looked, like parchment. In an instant, doubt vanished, and the two voices in her head united: *They cannot win. I will not be able to win here either. It is the wood, the metal, the*

32

blades, the oil, the flames — that last. It is the flesh and the spirit that are bowed and twisted for their purpose. Those warriors of myth and legend were invincible only in stories. Blood is spilt, flesh and bone are torn and shattered and burnt. Only the weapons remain unharmed: wood and metal gleaming as though smiling. The victory belongs to them. All the while we feared the hordes beyond; all the while they were among us here. And my parents, what is left of them?

When she spoke, her voice was steady and clear. And when she told them that she would not stay and work in the kitchen they did not try to persuade her. Her father turned on the fryer and her mother lit the range.

On the Sidewalk Bleeding

By Evan Hunter

The boy lay bleeding in the rain. He was sixteen years old, and he wore a bright purple silk jacket, and the lettering across the back of the jacket read THE ROYALS. The boy's name was Andy, and the name was written in black thread on the front of the jacket, just over the heart. *Andy*.

He had been stabbed ten minutes ago. The knife had entered just below his ribs, tearing a wide gap in his flesh. He lay on the sidewalk with the March rain drilling his jacket and drilling his body and washing away the blood that poured from his open wound. He had known terrible pain when the knife had torn across his body, then sudden relief when the blade was pulled away. He had heard the voice saying, 'That's for you, Royal!' and then the sound of footsteps hurrying into the rain, and then he had fallen to the sidewalk, clutching his stomach, trying to stop the flow of blood.

He tried to yell for help, but he had no voice. He did not know why his voice was gone, or why there was an open hole in his body from which his life ran redly. It was 11.30 p.m., but he did not know the time.

There was another thing he did not know.

He did not know he was dying. He lay on the sidewalk bleeding, and he thought only: *That was a fierce rumble. They got me good that time*, but he did not know he was dying. He would have been frightened had he known. He lay bleeding and wishing he could cry out for help, but there was no voice in his throat. There was only the bubbling of blood from between his lips whenever he opened his mouth to speak. He lay silent in his pain, waiting, waiting for someone to find him.

He could hear the sound of automobile tyres hushed on the rainswept streets, far away at the other end of the long alley. He could see the splash of neon at the other end of the alley. It was painting the pavement red and green.

He wondered if Laura would be angry.

He had left the jump to get a package of cigarettes. He had told her he would be back in a few minutes, and then he had gone downstairs and found the candy store closed. He knew that Alfredo's on the next block would be open. He had started through the alley, and that was when he'd been ambushed.

He could hear the faint sound of music now, coming from a long, long way off. He wondered if Laura was dancing, wondered if she had missed him yet. Maybe she thought he wasn't coming back. Maybe she thought he'd cut out for good. Maybe she'd already left the jump and gone home. He thought of her face, the brown eyes and the jet-black hair, and thinking of her he forgot his pain a little, forgot that blood was rushing from his body.

Someday he would marry Laura. Someday he would marry her, and they would have a lot of kids, and then they would get out of the neighbourhood. They would move to a clean project in the Bronx, or maybe they would move to Staten Island. When they were married, when they had kids.

He heard footsteps at the other end of the alley. He lifted his cheek from the sidewalk and looked into the darkness and tried to cry out, but again there was only a soft hissing bubble of blood on his mouth.

The man came down the alley. He had not seen Andy yet. He walked, and then stopped to lean against the brick of the building, and then walked again. He saw Andy then and came towards him, and he stood over him for a long time, the minutes ticking, ticking, watching him and not speaking.

Then he said, 'What's a matter, buddy?'

Andy could not speak, and he could barely move. He lifted his face slightly and looked up at the man. He smelled the sickening odour of alcohol. The man was drunk.

The man was smiling.

'Did you fall down, buddy?' he asked. 'You mus' be as drunk as I am.'

He squatted alongside Andy.

'You gonna catch cold here,' he said. 'What's a matter? You like layin' in the wet?'

Andy could not answer. The rain spattered around them.

'You like a drink?'

Andy shook his head.

'I gotta bottle. Here,' the man said. He pulled a pint bottle from his inside jacket pocket. Andy tried to move, but pain wrenched him back flat against the sidewalk.

'Take it,' the man said. He kept watching Andy. 'Take it.' When Andy did not move, he said, 'Nev' mind, I'll have one m'self.' He tilted the bottle to his lips, and then wiped the back of his hand across his mouth. 'You too young to be drinkin' anyway. Should be 'shamed of yourself, drunk an' laying in an alley, all wet. Shame on you. I gotta good minda calla cop.'

Andy nodded. Yes, he tried to say. Yes, call a cop. Please. Call one.

'Oh, you don't like that, huh?' the drunk said. 'You don' wanna cop to fin' you all drunk an' wet in an alley, huh? Okay, buddy. This time you get off easy.' He got to his feet. 'This time you lucky,' he said. He waved broadly at Andy, and then almost lost his footing. 'S'long, buddy,' he said.

Wait, Andy thought. *Wait please, I'm bleeding.*

'S'long,' the drunk said again. 'I see you aroun',' and then he staggered off up the alley.

Andy lay and thought: *Laura, Laura. Are you dancing?*

The couple came into the alley suddenly. They ran into the alley together, running from the rain. The boy held the girl's elbow, the girl spreading a newspaper over her head to protect her hair. Andy watched them run into the alley laughing, and then duck into the doorway not ten feet from him.

'Man, what rain!' the boy said. 'You could drown out there.'

'I have to get home,' the girl said. 'It's late, Freddie. I have to get home.'

'We got time,' Freddie said. 'Your people won't raise a fuss if you're a little late. Not with this kind of weather.'

'It's dark,' the girl said, and she giggled.

'Yeah,' the boy answered, his voice very low.

'Freddie . . . ?'

'Um?'

'You're . . . you're standing very close to me.'

'Um.'

There was a long silence. Then the girl said, 'Oh,' only that single word, and Andy knew she'd been kissed. He suddenly hungered for Laura's mouth. It was then that he wondered if he would ever kiss Laura again. It was then that he wondered if he was dying.

No, he thought, *I can't be dying, not from a little street rumble, not from just getting cut. Guys get cut all the time in rumbles. I can't be dying. No, that's stupid. That don't make sense at all.*

'You shouldn't,' the girl said.

'Why not?'

'I don't know.'

'Do you like it?'

'Yes.'

'So?'

'I don't know.'

'I love you, Angela,' the boy said.

'I love you, too, Freddie,' the girl said, and Andy listened and thought: *I love you, Laura. Laura, I think maybe I'm dying. Laura, this is stupid but I think I'm dying. Laura, I think I'm dying!*

He tried to speak. He tried to move. He tried to crawl towards the doorway. He tried to make a noise, a sound, and a grunt came from his lips. He tried again, and another grunt came, a low animal grunt of pain.

'What was that?' the girl said, breaking away from the boy.

'I don't know,' he answered.

'Go look, Freddie.'

'No. Wait.'

Andy moved his lips again. Again the sound came from him.

'Freddie!'

'What?'

'I'm scared.'

'I'll go see,' the boy said.

He stepped into the alley. He walked over to where Andy lay on the ground. He stood over him, watching him.

'You all right?' he asked.

'What is it?' Angela said from the doorway.

'Somebody's hurt,' Freddie said.

'Let's get out of here,' Angela said.

'No. Wait a minute.' He knelt down beside Andy. 'You cut?' he asked.

Andy nodded. The boy kept looking at him. He saw the lettering on the jacket then. THE ROYALS. He turned to Angela.

'He's a Royal,' he said.

'Let's . . . what . . . what do you want to do, Freddie?'

'I don't know. I don't want to get mixed up in this. He's a Royal. We help him, and the Guardians'll be down on our necks. I don't want to get mixed up in this, Angela.'

'Is he . . . is he hurt bad?'

'Yeah, it looks that way.'

'What shall we do?'

'I don't know.'

'We can't leave him here in the rain.' Angela hesitated. 'Can we?'

'If we get a cop, the Guardians'll find out who,' Freddie said. 'I don't know, Angela, I don't know.'

Angela hesitated a long time before answering. Then she said, 'I have to go home, Freddie. My people will begin to worry.'

'Yeah,' Freddie said. He looked at Andy again. 'You all right?' he asked. Andy lifted his face from the sidewalk, and his eyes said: *Please, please help me*, and maybe Freddie read what his eyes were saying, and maybe he didn't.

Behind him, Angela said, 'Freddie, let's get out of here! Please!' Freddie stood up. He looked at Andy again, and then mumbled, 'I'm sorry.' He took Angela's arm, and together they ran towards the neon splash at the other end of the alley.

Why, they're afraid of the Guardians, Andy thought in amazement. *But why shouldn't they be? I wasn't afraid of the Guardians. I never turkeyed out of a rumble with the Guardians. I got heart. But I'm bleeding.*

The rain was soothing. It was a cold rain, but his body was hot all over, and the rain helped cool him. He had always liked rain. He could remember sitting in Laura's house one time, the rain running down the windows, and just looking out over the street, watching the people running from the rain. That was when he'd first joined the Royals. He could remember how happy he was the Royals had taken him. The Royals and the Guardians, two of the biggest. He was a Royal. There had been meaning to the title.

Now, in the alley, with the cold rain washing his hot body, he wondered about the meaning. If he died, he was Andy. He was not a Royal. He was simply Andy, and he was dead. And he wondered suddenly if the Guardians who had ambushed him and knifed him had ever once realised he was Andy? Had they known that he was Andy, or had they simply known that he was a Royal wearing a purple silk jacket? Had they stabbed *him*, Andy, or had they only stabbed the jacket and the title, and what good was the title if you were dying?

I'm Andy, he screamed wordlessly. *I'm Andy*.

An old lady stopped at the other end of the alley. The garbage cans were stacked there, beating noisily in the rain. The old lady carried an umbrella with broken ribs, carried it like a queen. She stepped into the mouth of the alley, shopping bag over one arm. She lifted the lids of the garbage cans. She did not hear Andy grunt because she was a little deaf and because the rain was beating on the cans. She collected her string and her newspapers, and an old hat with a feather on it from one of the garbage cans, and a broken footstool from another of the cans. And then she replaced the lids and lifted her umbrella high and walked out of the alley mouth. She had worked quickly and soundlessly, and now she was gone.

The alley looked very long now. He could see people passing at the other end of it, and he wondered who the people were, and he wondered if he would ever get to know them, wondered who it was on the Guardians who had stabbed him, who had plunged the knife into his body.

'That's for you, Royal!' the voice had said. 'That's for you, Royal!' Even in his pain, there had been some sort of pride in knowing he was a Royal. Now there was no pride at all. With the rain beginning to chill him, with the blood pouring steadily between his fingers, he knew only a sort of dizziness. He could only think: *I want to be Andy.*

It was not very much to ask of the world.

He watched the world passing at the other end of the alley. The world didn't know he was Andy. The world didn't know he was alive. He wanted to say, 'Hey, I'm alive! Hey, look at me! I'm alive! Don't you know I'm alive? Don't you know I exist?'

He felt weak and very tired. He felt alone and wet and feverish and chilled. He knew he was going to die now. That made him suddenly sad. He was filled with sadness that his life would be over at sixteen. He felt at once as if he had never done anything, never been anywhere. There were so many things to do. He wondered why he'd never thought of them before, wondered why the rumbles and the jumps and the purple jackets had always seemed so important to him before. Now they seemed like such small things in a world he was missing, a world that was rushing past at the other end of the alley.

I don't want to die, he thought. *I haven't lived yet.*

It seemed very important to him that he take off the purple jacket. He was very close to dying, and when they found him, he did not want them to say, 'Oh, it's a Royal.' With great effort, he rolled over on to his back. He felt the pain tearing at his stomach when he moved. If he never did another thing, he wanted to take off the jacket. The jacket had only one meaning now, and that was a very simple meaning.

If he had not been wearing the jacket, he wouldn't have been stabbed. The knife had not been plunged in hatred of Andy. The knife hated only the purple jacket. The jacket was a stupid meaningless thing that was robbing him of his life.

He lay struggling with the shiny wet jacket. His arms were heavy. Pain ripped fire across his body whenever he moved. But he squirmed and fought and twisted until one arm was free and then the other. He rolled away from the jacket and lay quite still, breathing heavily, listening to the sound of his breathing and the sounds of the rain and thinking: *Rain is sweet, I'm Andy.*

She found him in the doorway a minute past midnight. She left the dance to look for him. When she found him she knelt beside him and said, 'Andy, it's me, Laura.'

He did not answer her. She backed away from him, tears springing into her eyes, and then she ran from the alley. She did not stop running until she found a cop.

And now, standing with the cop, she looked down at him. The cop rose and said, 'He's dead.' All the crying was out of her now. She stood in the rain and said nothing, looking at the dead boy on the pavement, and looking at the purple jacket that rested a foot away from his body.

The cop picked up the jacket and turned it over in his hands.

'A Royal, huh?' he said.

She looked at the cop, and, very quietly, she said, 'His name is Andy.'

The cop slung the jacket over his arm. He took out his black pad, and he flipped it open to a blank page.

'A Royal,' he said.

Then he began writing.

Invisible Mass of the Back Row

By Claudette Williams

I stand in the middle of the room, surrounded by anxious faces. It is my turn to recite the day's lesson. The Inspector's ruler points to me.

'Stand up. Recite the adventures of Columbus. What was the date of Columbus' landing in Jamaica? What were the names of his ships? Why was he in the Caribbean?'

My heart pounds. The heat of the morning sun, soaking through the galvanised roof, is magnified inside the schoolroom. The stench of fear is in everyone's nostrils. Something tells me that my days of being hidden, disposed of, dispatched to the invisibility of the back row, are numbered.

I stand up, my limbs shaking uncontrollably, sweat dripping from my armpits, my eyes inflamed. My belly aches. I am petrified. Words fail to come out. They are formed in my head, but my lips do not speak them. The Inspector's eyes pierce me through. They demand a response, demand to be respected and obeyed.

'What was Columbus doing here anyway?' The trapped words inside my head tumble out. The rebel inside me is alive. The schoolroom becomes even quieter, if that is possible.

'You in for it,' Patricia, sitting next to where I stand shaking, mutters without moving her lips. I know she is speaking the truth.

The Inspector's face is frozen. Miss Henderson, form six teacher, pounces with the ruler. Her face says she is sure she could not have heard what she thought she heard.

'What did you say, Hortense?'

From I don't know where, a power surges through me. My fists clench. My teeth lock into each other. Miss Henderson reads challenge in my face. I stand still, not daring to say any more.

'What did you say?' she commands, challenging me to repeat my *facetiness*. And again it happens. Words gush out of my mouth. 'Is what Columbus did want? Who invite him here?'

Before the last word has left my lips, the sharp sting of the ruler cracks my knuckles. Stupidly, I had left my clenched fist on the desk in front of me. The blow brings me back to the steam bath. Sweat now drips from my face, floods my armpits, drips from between my legs.

I could kill this woman with her sharp pointed nose, mean eyes and frightened face. We cross eyes, and for an instant I see the fear which has trapped us in this rank, smelly room. Miss Henderson is afraid. She is as much afraid of the Inspector as I am.

My brains, what brains I have left, are bouncing around in my skull, goading me on. I will get more of the ruler. It is written across Miss Henderson's wrinkled forehead. My life is at an end! At least in this school. If Miss Henderson does not kill me with this ruler, my aunt is sure to finish me off when she hears how I back-chat the Inspector and Teacher Henderson.

My parents are in England and living with my aunt is like walking a tight-rope. One little slip and I am in big trouble. Dis look and smell like big trouble to me.

The lunch bell echoes throughout the school. My salvation? For now, anyway.

Hungry bellies rumble in the steam bath, but we are still transfixed by the Inspector, paralysed by Miss

Henderson's stare. Feet shuffle, fingers scratch prickly skin. From outside there is the freedom of released bodies bouncing against the partition and liberated voices rising. They magnify our imprisonment. But the walls have been breached. The jailers are quick to realise that this battle is lost. For now.

'Class dismissed,' the Inspector grudgingly commands. Miss Henderson lowers her eyes.

'Good afternoon, Inspector. Good afternoon, Miss Henderson,' we recite. Miss Henderson steps aside, stiffly. Fifty tense bodies scurry past, politely, straining to taste the fresh, if hot air of the noon-day world and feed themselves from the lunch women under the cotton tree. But first there is Lorna Phillips to take care of. Somebody has to pay for this.

'Yo red pickney always sit a de front of de class. Unno t'ink is because yu pretty. Is only 'cause teacher frighten fi yu pupa,' I curse Lorna, as we bundle down the steps, out of earshot of Miss Henderson and the Inspector.

'Is 'cause yu black and stupid why teacher meck yu sit a de back all de time,' Lorna chirps in.

'Is who you calling stupid? Yo want yu bloody nose right here?'

This is always the outcome of a tense morning in school. A fight often follows the Inspector's visits.

Lorna pushes past me and tries to make a break for the school gate. But I give chase, followed by Samuel, Tim, Patricia, Maud and Yvonne. Today she will pay for being teacher's favourite, for being 'red', for being rich, for having everything I don't have.

'Look how fast she moving on dem marga foot,' taunts Yvonne.

'Come, let we beat her up,' I shout, and we surge forward, pursuing Lorna out of school.

I might not know the answers, but I can fight.

Just then, from behind the school gate, Teacher Edwards comes into view. He is big, sturdy and beautifully dark, with a baby moustache. He is handsomely dressed in his Dashiki suit. There is a kindness about this man that is not usually found among teachers. He would always listen to you, and not just take the teacher's side. He only beat you if he really feel you was out of order, rude, or you get catch with something you thief. We respected and even liked him.

The running stops, slows to a polite walk. The hot pursuit melts into fixed grins and prim steps.

'Good afternoon, children.'

'Good afternoon, Teacher Edwards,' we still the vengeance in our voices long enough to chant in unison.

Lorna makes the most of Teacher Edwards' presence.

Walking as fast as she could, she says her polite good afternoon and makes a beeline for the hill which distances her from the rest of us. She is safe this time. We turn down the hill.

'Meck she gone. We'll get her tomorrow,' we plot. My voice and limbs quiet down. For the first time that day, my heartbeat falls back into its normal silent rhythm. There is always tomorrow.

It is the pain of the Inspector that has fuelled my blood; the pain of the ruler was nothing. Chu, mi use to beatings. One little ruler slap a nothing. But dat renking, facety man. A way him come from? Dis warra warra man, jus' a bother people head. Him 'now de score. After all him is suppose to be black.

47

My uncle say all a dem collude to humiliate, not just me, but all a we, all de people who look like me. All de poor black people dem. Meck him no pick pan de red pickney dem, a meck him t'ink say is we alone no know nothing.

I walk silently down the hill with the others. Each of us is distracted by our own thoughts and anger at the morning. Food hunger is temporarily forgotten. Lorna Phillips and de Inspector dem all de same. Have plenty of money and hate we.

At the bottom of the hill, we are nourished by a wealth of warm, familiar sights and smells. The lunch women come into view. They are always there, big and strong, jutting out from the base of the towering cotton tree. Miss Ivy, as always, has on her red tie-head. In the afternoon sun, as she sits on her three-legged stool, it makes her face glow. Her food box is secured between her legs.

Aunt Dine always smells of cinnamon. You know her smell, because if you dare to make her laugh and expose her bare toothless black gums, in quiet moments she will give you a big smothering hug. Her missing teeth give her face a funny, quaint look. She is never scary to us because she lives in our district and we know her.

Miss Mavis always sits to the right of Aunt Dine, because, she says, she is practising to be on the right hand side of her Maker. Miss Mavis has the most beautifully oiled, ivory coloured skin in the whole world, and white, white eyes which twinkle and wink at you when she talks. She is never cross for long, but will cuss you out one minute and tell you scriptures the next. Her face is electric, whirling and changing as she speaks. Her eyes search your face for understanding.

48

And then there is one-foot Herby who is always late with his sky-juice and snowball. He can argue, always on about 'de dam hot sun,' which is, 'good for nothing, and only melting him ice, quick, quick, o'clock.'

The boxes are unwrapped. Our senses are assaulted by saltfish fritters, fried dumplings, red herring, corn-meal pudding, sweet potato pudding, oranges, plums, mangoes or sugar-cane, snowball and sky-juice. Smells mingle and whirl, creating a comfortable oasis under the gigantic cotton tree. That same tree serves as a lover's nest and gambling spot at nights. If trees could talk, what stories this one would tell!

We go down the hill. The gloom of humiliation, the pain of the assault on all of us, lifts. We search for our lunch money and think of food. Like swarming bees we descend, shouting our orders to the lunch women.

'Unny stop de noise and wait. How many han' yu t'ink we have?' Miss Mavis quietly reprimands.

The shouts subside only for a moment as we change our orders and surge again.

'Two penny worth of dumpling and saltfish, please Miss Mavis.'

'Mi only want fritters.'

'Mi jus' want a piece of cornmeal pudding today.'

'But Aunt Dine dat red herring so little bit.'

'Yu have no crackers again Miss Ivy?'

'How come Herby teck so long fi share de ice?'

The clutter and bustle carry on until the sweat is running down the women's faces. Wash-rags, carried on shoulders like a uniform, mop brows, as they try to keep track of orders and change.

'Lord unny pickney is somet'ing else. Unny gone like nobody no feed unny. Dem mus' a wok unny hard a school today.'

The chatter waves and heaves. The banter and retort goes backwards and forwards until the lunch money secured in pockets and knotted in handkerchiefs has been spent for the day.

Boxes are empty. We mingle, swap and taste each other's purchases, eat, talk with mouths full. As we drift away, so do Aunt Mavis, Aunt Dine and Miss Ivy. Herby is the last to pack up and vacate the cotton tree. The forces have been spent for the day.

Will I one day move from the back row? Would I be let off from reciting the day's lesson, because I know it, just once? Would it ever be my turn to sit at the front, and not have to answer the Inspector's questions?

The house is buzzing. A letter and a big, big parcel have arrived from England. 'Me mother sending for we. Me and me two brothers going to England.' I sang, 'Me a go a Englan'. Me mumma and puppa send fi we.' Dat will show Lorna Phillips. She have no people in a Englan'. Columbus can get lost. No more standing up in the middle of the class. No more hot, sweaty classroom. No more Teacher Henderson. No more Inspector. Me a go a Englan'.

November sixteenth. It is dark outside. Night creatures are going to sleep. Day animals still don't know it is time to wake up. Inside, the lamp is lit, casting its honey glow on our faces still dazed with sleep.

'Unno go wash, and put on unno clothes,' Salna orders. Sleepily, we obey.

The sun is creeping over Easington hills, reflecting the honey glow inside. Its full power is still waiting to wake up. I cannot drink any tea, cannot eat what is to be my last piece of hard-dough bread and butter. My stomach is tight. My jaws are refusing to chew on this familiar taste.

'If yu don't want de tea, lef' it an go put on yu clothes. Dem all dey pon de chair, and don't mess up de hair,' I am ordered again. I do as I am told. No time for back-chatting.

Now there is much coming and going. In the dim light of morning, not yet fully awake, neighbours come to say farewell. They bring parting gifts of mangoes, and presents for relatives in England, not seen or heard from in many years.

Like a stranger, I greet my new clothes, gingerly feeling, inhaling the new cloth smells. I try to work out which piece to put on first without disturbing my newly crafted hairstyle.

I dress in silence, only now beginning to fully realise. Today, my every action, in this dim morning light, is to be registered in the cosmos as my last in this familiar, tiny, two-roomed house.

We pile into the van just as the morning sun claims its place in the sky. It releases its passions and burns away the last stillness of the night. The silence of parting quiets the most active tongue. The drive to the airport is long and hot. Still, the pain of parting traps us in our silent world.

Who will look after Cousy's grave? Who will make sure that the weeds do not choke her roses?

Cousy had not moved, as she always did, when the sun peeped over the hill top. Had not roused me to do my morning chores when night kiss morning awake. I thought Cousy's coldness was just the passing of night.

So I slept on, not noticing that her 'old bones', as she often referred to herself, had not stirred, that her limbs were stiff, that she got colder as the morning got warmer.

Lloyd banging on the door, ordering me to get up and feed de chickens, alerted the yard. I woke to find Cousy's gentle face tight and still, a trickle of tears running from her opened eyes.

'Why are you crying Cousy?' I asked as I crept sleepily out of bed. There was no reply. And I found myself crying too. Her stillness, her unfocused stare, signalled a change.

I opened the door to find the whole yard gathered outside, waiting. They understood the signals. Death had crept under the door and taken Cousy away in her sleep.

'I want Cousy,' I hollered, as I fell into Miss Olive's arms.

Does this mean I won't ever again share Cousy's bed and snuggle into her warm bosom? Won't smell her old mysterious smells, and watch her crinkled face?

Now, this thought forces out the hot salty tears which well up inside. I am leaving her behind. The tears flow freely, soiling my newly polished face. Bringing me back to the speeding van taking me away from Heartease, from Cousy, from my goats, from Lorna Phillips. Towards . . . the gigantic, shimmering aeroplanes.

The sun releases all its enormous strength. The sea retaliates. It shimmers its bluest blue, a blue that envelops the airport and the parked aeroplanes.

The following hours are filled with a numbness. The only parallels I can think of are visits to the dentist with anaesthetic injected to deaden the pain or when you freshly buck your toe on a big rock stone. My inside is dead. I am cold in the blazing sunshine.

Now, everybody is crying, some pretending that they aren't. Handkerchiefs flap goodbye and wipe streaming eyes. My brothers and I are ceremoniously handed over to a pretty, chocolate-coloured woman dressed in a blue uniform. We follow her, reluctantly, into places of strangeness, places with strange lights and strange demands. People smile knowingly and gather up our belongings.

Then we are sitting in the belly of the gigantic metal bird, which we have only seen before from the ground, looking upwards. This is it. We are going to England.

England brings my mother and father back to me. It drags them forward from the fragile recesses of my young memory. I remember snippets of incidents which had told me of their existence. How long have we been separated? Well, it is hard to know. It was hard, those days long ago, to understand what was going on. I cannot count how many days I was without my father's company, nor am I positive of the many years without my mother's embrace. But memory surges suggest seven years, perhaps, without father and five without mother.

I was not to know then, that although I would return many times, that first departure was the beginning of my exile from Heartease.

Paraffin heaters
smell
always just coming
into cold dark places
afraid and
excited at the same
time
cold
smell

wanting to be elsewhere
in fact Jamaica

'Yes, Salna,' I replied for the tenth time, to my mother's call from the kitchen. A pokey, steamy place at the back of a cold, cold house.

All the houses I see are stuck together, with no place to play outside, no yard. Do children not play outside in this England? Is it always so cold? Does it ever get warm? Does the sun shine here?

'Now, listen to me child,' my mother's dark, youthful face smiles down at me, brings me back to the steamy place. I sit huddled in strange clothes, close to the paraffin heater. 'You had better decide what you are going to call me. You can choose from Mother, Mummy, Mum. The same goes for your father. You've got Dad, Daddy or Father to choose from.'

This little talk put an end to days of nervous tension about deciding what to call my England parents. Having arrived, what do you call these newly acquired people? I dreaded answering to my mother's call. What do you answer when strangers call to you, but they are not strangers really, they are your mother and father? I fell back on old responses, familiar language.

No one told me I would need a new language in dis England.

'My mother who dey a England; my mother who a send fa me in a England.' Here I was without a language to reply to her calls. Lorna Phillips, I still hate you, but oh I wish you were here. At least I know your name.

Mum came with me for my interview at Devon Spencer School. She sat right next to me as I read for the Headmistress. I read but did not know the words of this new language, could not read the words of this strange book. I did my best. I read until I was told to stop, being corrected by the Headmistress. The Headmistress was impressed. I was impressed. My Mum was impressed. My impressive reading enrolled me in one five, the hottest, baddest stream in the first year, only second to one six, the remedial stream.

My strategic location in one five has a familiar feel about it. There is no Lorna Phillips. In this group we have all recently arrived, from one island or another but mostly from Jamaica and all poor, clearly black and one rung from the back row, the bottom stream. This is home away from home. I simply settle down to school life and cultivate the culture of the back row. We graduate in hair plaiting, make up and cussing. Our section of the common-room is dominated by the smell of hair pomander, face powder and Woolworth's latest perfume fragrances.

'You know say Columbus enslave de Indian dem fine in the islands. De same one dem who save him life, and help him restock him ships and tell him say him no reach India yet.' Joycelin is feeding us information as she leafs through her latest book, discovered at the local library.

'You lie!' The challenge comes from Fay Green. 'Because is Africans dem enslave and ship to de islands, to slave on sugar plantations, fi make sugar fi white people tea in a England.'

The hair on the back of my neck stands up. The room is suddenly very hot. This man, Columbus keeps coming back to haunt me.

'With all de tea dem drink in dis place, is we still a fi meck sugar fi dem fi sweeten it,' says Joycelin as she continues to leaf through the book, stopping every so often to throw out morsels about the exploits of slavers, life on plantations and the fights slaves and the indigenous

Indians waged for their freedom. Conversations weave and heave. We move back and forth between anger, total disbelief and downright outrage.

'Is who write dat book you reading? 'Cause is foolishness you telling me. I don't believe a word of it,' Fay Green finally bursts out.

Each new piece of information is challenged and questioned. We discover heroes, rebels, guerrilla fighters. They help us assert our right to be. Toussaint L'Ouverture, Sojourner Truth, Nanny, Cudjoe, Paul Bogle. The books tell us they all come from our own back yard. Thoughts of them mingle with the hair oils, face powder, and self-affirmation lessons which claim space in our section of the common-room.

Group humiliation replaces individual humiliation here in England schools. This bottom from remedial class gets the meanest, most feared teachers in the school. Their sole intention seem to be to ensure that we know and keep our place. And Columbus keeps coming up. Today's lesson is to make sure we have learnt the lesson of conquest.

Things mingle and whirl in my mind. Easington heat. Easington sweat. English cold. English ice. Frozen faces, frozen information, frozen places.

'Why did Columbus sail to the Indies in 1493, Hortense?' The frozen face cracks momentarily. 'And while you are thinking of the answer, Fay Green you can be thinking of the commodities which Hawkins traded with the Portuguese of the Gold Coast of Africa.'

Indignantly, the back row comes into its own. 'Columbus was looking for a new route to India, so that when he landed in the Caribbean he was good and lost; he thought he was in India. The people who befriended him were massacred and the rest enslaved to mine gold and cultivate sugar. When they died from diseases Europeans brought to the islands, they were replaced by Africans stolen from the Gold Coast of Africa, Miss.'

I said all of this slowly, so that I would say it well. Some of it came out just as I had read it in a book that one of the others had taken from the local library. Slowly, but quickly, because my head was hot and heavy. I can feel the others in the back row feeling proud. We watch the frozen face thaw out. We watch her eyes travel right along the two rows at the back. We watch a stream of red blood rush from the neck to the top of her head.

Fay Green cannot hold her voice back. 'Hawkins traded trinkets for black African people, who were enslaved and shipped to the Caribbean to slave on sugar plantations, to make sugar for English people's tea, Miss.'

All eyes are on the teacher. The back row is tense, wanting an explosion.

The school pips signal the end of the lesson and class five, unusually dignified, stands up and leaves the room. Miss remains fixed to her chair.

Whoops and slaps are heard down the corridor. The back row claims a victory. 'She won't be asking us those stupid questions again, will she?'

Voices are raised, claiming, proclaiming, learning the new language in dis here England.

Deeper than Colour

By Ijeoma Inyama

God! Miss Halpern, our English teacher, is well renk! She reckons our class would be '*much more productive*' if we weren't sat with our friends. So she moves us about and makes us sit with people she *knows* we'd never sit with through choice. She's vex me *twice*, man! First of all, you don't expect to get treated like a first year when you're in the *fifth* year − I mean, her idea of a seating arrangement is well antiquated! And secondly, she's taken me from my spars, man! Ever since the second year, I've sat next to Heather Phillips, in front of Antoinette Varley and Takesha Brown. Now barely into the first term of the fifth and we get split up!

'Nadine Charles, I want you to sit next to John Danucci in front of my desk.'

Now she's vexed me four times, no, make that five. Sitting next to Danucci *and* in the front row. I can't believe it! Neither can the rest of the class. *Everyone* knows we're the worst pairing ever.

Let me explain some simple rudimentary classroom psychology, while I grab up my books and cuss my way down the aisle. See, I'm no roughneck, but I love my ragga and jungle . . . like the girls I go round with − Heather, Antoinette and Takesha. So naturally we get friendly with like-minded guys. Horace Batchelor's an example. 'Cept for Horace, the guys ain't true ragamuffins, but they do get a roughneck reputation 'cause they like ragga. Being Black helps. And if you can run the lyrics . . . well, you're talking god-like status.

But let me get back to Danucci. He hangs out with the 'trendies'. We call them the *Kiss FM posse*. They're into 'British soul' and buy their clothes from 'Hyper' – anything that's the latest t'ing. I mean, if it was thrashing two dustbin lids together, them lot'd be into that, no danger. So, us lot stick to ourselves, them lot do likewise – and never the twain shall meet stylee. I mean, if I went to some roughneck ragga sound dressed like them freaky deakies – some Barbarella meets and rough up Miss Marple kind of doo-lah I'd get nuff comments!

It must sound like something out of *West Side Story*, the Jets versus the Sharks. But it ain't. We don't have gang fights. Just a mutual understanding that we don't have nothing to do with each other. And that's why me and Danucci are the worst pairing Miss Halpern could have made.

A ragga-loving, hardcore jungle *gyal* ain't got nothing decent to say to a trendy freaky deaky.

At morning break my situation is the focus of the playground discussion. Horace reckons that Miss Halpern needs '*hormone treatment*', or a good kick up the back-side, or both, for what she's done. Then he hits on me!

'. . . and don't get no ideas!'

'Yeah, and I'm *really* your girlfriend, ain't I?' I snap. 'Besides, I couldn't go out with no freaky deakster. I'd be too shamed up to walk down the street with him!'

Horace has asked me out twice and twice I've turned him down. Truth is, I'd be too shamed up to walk down the street with *him*! I can't stand the way he's always got to have a comb in his miserable head – but does he ever use it? Now OK, I wouldn't get on the cover of *Black Hair & Beauty* (Takesha could easy), but I could sneak in between. So what makes a guy with no class, style, the personality of a crusty old pair of Y-fronts and looks that would make Godzilla a hunk think that I'd be interested in him? Try and explain that to Horace Batchelor. I've tried, but he won't listen. He reckons I'm the one for him. God knows why.

★ ★ ★

Two weeks and six English lessons have passed and I'm still sitting next to Danucci. I give him dirty looks, run down *Kiss FM* loud enough for him to hear and make sure my books cover at least half his desk. He ain't said a word to me. Maybe he's scared of Horace. But it really annoys me 'cause it's like I'm not there! He shares jokes and raves about the latest rare groove with his trendy pals – and they all sit around me, which I can't stand. And he exchanges loving glances with his girlfriend, Debra Haynes. She sits in the back row, two seats away from Heather. You've got to see this girl. She thinks she's *it*, her nose up in the air or looking down it at you. She's well facety! She thinks she's so hip in her clothes, but she always looks like she's wearing the clothes her grand-mother gave her; which is probably the case.

Well, all that I can take. But then today Miss Halpern tells us she wants us to write a short story based on some aspect of our lives. Creative writing's got to be the thing I hate most. I get bored after writing one line! Anyway, she goes on and on about how she wants us to use '. . . *research as a means of getting information about your backgrounds* . . .' Which really means, bug your parents for the next seven days. I can't be bothered with all that. But Danucci and his crew think it's a great idea. Typical!

On our way home from school that afternoon, a crowd of us stopped by the newsagent's, ignoring the ten-foot-high sign that reads 'ONLY TWO KIDS AT A TIME'. And Danucci's in there with a couple of his trendy mates.

Hassle time!

Horace accidentally-on-purpose knocks into Danucci, whose nose is stuck in a music magazine. Danucci don't even glance up – Horace is well miffed. Then Takesha shoves me into Danucci and he almost drops the magazine. He glares at me. I'd never noticed his sparkling green eyes, his curly black eyelashes and . . .

'Nadine!'

My friends are all looking at me like I've grown a moustache or something. Danucci goes up to the counter with his mates to pay for the magazine. But not before giving me a look that could've had me ten foot under. For the first time I realize that he hates me as much as I hate him.

★ ★ ★

Talk about stress me out! I've got Miss Halpern on my back about that stupid short story I haven't written. Heather, Antoinette and Takesha on my back about fancying Danucci, and Horace on my back about going out with him. Well, before I crack up, I'm going to have one last go at getting some order into my life. '*Deal with each problem one at a time*' is my mum's favourite saying. First on my list is getting that story written.

Normally I never go near a library. Man, I break out in a cold sweat just thinking about one! But I force myself. The assignment's due in on Thursday and that's tomorrow! So in I go, on my own. I could've gone in with Antoinette and Takesha, as they love the library, but they'd already done their assignments. Heather *never* does assignments and she has the same aversion to libraries as I do – serious intellectual atmosphere, ughh!

I go straight upstairs to the study area. There are 'nuff kids in here, man! Swotting at the *beginning* of term? That's well sad, man! It's hunt for a seat time. I make my way past the tables. *No one was talking.* Can you believe that? Noses stuck in books. Disgusting! Ah-ha, a seat right by the window at the back. I could get away with eating my Mars bar without the crusty librarian seeing me. A freckle-faced, ginger-haired girl heads towards my seat. I throw myself into it. She gives me a filthy look and stomps off.

So I get out my exercise book and my Biros and take in the other kids around the table. Sangita, who's in the year below me; she lives in the library apparently. Tunde, a really quiet guy in my year – and the cleverest, Cheryl Watson, also in my year and a bookworm and . . . oh no! Danucci!

It's too late to move – there's nowhere else to sit. So I stay there silently cursing myself – 'til he looks up and sees me. (He'd had his head down in a computer book. That assignment's not due in 'til next month!) He kind of scowls at me, then returns to his book.

I can't concentrate on my story – it's that awkward. Ten minutes have gone by without us saying a word. This is driving me mad! I've got to say something!

'Look, I'm sorry about the other day in the newsagent's, but it weren't my fault.'

He looks at me, stunned, like he must've been preparing himself for aggro or something, particularly since none of his friends is around. But he still doesn't say anything.

'I said, I apologize. What d'you want, blood?' I hate being made to feel uncomfortable.

'Why?'

I can't work the boy out. 'Why what?'

'Why are you saying you're sorry when we both know you don't mean it?'

'Hey, you ain't in my head, so you don't know what's going on in there. But if you must know, I don't never say nothing that I don't mean. "*Better to offend than pretend*" is my motto.'

He folds his arms across his chest, looking triumphant. 'Not so hard without your mates, eh?'

'Neither are you.'

'I don't bother you, but you're *always* bothering me.'

A librarian nearby tells us to be quiet, so we are for about half a minute. Then he goes: 'Is that your English assignment?'

I stop doodling on the page. 'Nah, I'm designing a hi-tech kitchen for my mum's birthday present.'

The librarian is glowering at us.

'So what's it going to be about?' Danucci asks.

'How the hell do I know?'

He's getting as narked as I am, and I feel my conscience prickling . . .

'I don't know what to write,' I whisper. 'I don't know *how* to write.'

'It's easy. Write about what you know.'

'Oh yeah? As easy as that? So what did you write about then?'

So Danucci tells me his short story. But he has to tell me outside 'cause we get kicked out.

Massimo, the guy in his story, is about eight or nine.
He teases – no – bullies is more like it, his next-door
neighbour's son Haresh, who's around two years
younger. He'd call him 'paki' and stuff 'cause that's what
all his friends at school did, bully Black and Asian kids. It
was a mainly White school. Anyway, one day, Massimo's
grandad Alfonso (I love the names) came to visit,
overheard the name-calling and abuse and ordered
Massimo inside. Alfonso told Massimo how hard it was
for him being an Italian immigrant in the late thirties and
forties because of Mussolini and that and also because
he was well dark, being Sicilian. He told Massimo that
he was shaming him by insulting Haresh. Massimo felt
really bad because he loved his grandad (basically
because he spoilt him rotten). Then Massimo ended up
in a secondary school which was racially mixed and he
had no problem forming friendships which rivalled the
UN in their racial and cultural diversity.

'Our school's nothing like the UN.'

'So you guessed Massimo is based on me.'

'Just call me Einstein.'

He laughs.

'There's no way I could write like that.'

'Sure you can. Write about what you know.'

I look at him. 'I don't get it. Why are you helping me?'

He's about to answer when I spot my spars coming
out of McDonald's. I freeze. Danucci sighs. 'You want me
to disappear, right?'

They'll see us any time soon. So I goes, 'Well, you'd
do the same.'

He's got that same look he had in the newsagent's.
'Would I?' And he crosses the street in a huff just as they
spot me.

★ ★ ★

The past three days have been a bummer, an all-time low. Oh, I got my assignment done and handed it in on time, no worries there. Except that it's crap. No, it's my friends that have been stressing me out – big time – with the Danucci thing. They've been saying that I'll be trading in Redrat for Jamiroquai. Yesterday, Horace got me so vexed that I cussed him about his nappy-never-see-comb head. As for Danucci, he won't so much as look at me. Worst of all, that's what's bugging me the most! I know now why I hated him so much. I was *making* myself hate him because I knew I *liked* him. But now with him ignoring me I feel so depressed I can't eat or sleep let alone think properly.

Enough is enough! I'm going to sort this mess out. So I write him a note and put it in his desk before English class. If he still wants to know, he'll meet me by the huts after class.

★ ★ ★

'Ain't you afraid to be seen in public with me?'

I shrug my shoulders. I know he's pleased I left him that note. His green eyes are twinkling like crazy.

'I want to apologize.'

'Like last time?'

'You're making this really difficult.'

He leans against the wall. 'Good. You really pissed me off the other day.'

'I know and I've been suffering since.'

'Friends giving you a hard time?'

'*You're* giving me a hard time.'

Silence. I count the stripes on my hi-tops; one, two, three . . .

'I've always liked you Nadine.' He says it so softly.

'I'd never have guessed.'

'And as you wrote me a note . . .'

'Yeah, I like you, too. I guess I was trying to hide it by giving you a hard time.'

He smiles at me. 'I ain't saying it's going to be easy if we're friendly-like, my friends'll give me a hard time, too, you know. But I would never cross the street if they saw me with you. It depends on how much you want to be part of the crowd.'

'I've been really miserable since that day, I feel like I'd be living a lie if I kept . . . you know, pretending.'

'Better to offend than pretend, right?'

'Is Debra Haynes your girlfriend?'

He shakes his head. 'Is Horace Batchelor your boyfriend?'

I roll my eyes.

Then he pulls me close to him and we kiss. Then he puts his arm around me as we head towards the playground, where everyone will see us! I ain't going to lie and say I feel a hundred per cent comfortable about it. But for my own peace of mind, I've got to give it a go. Especially since I've just written a short story about it. I mean, it's got to be a first in our school: a ragga-loving junglis girl going with a trendy freaky deak.

The Ones who Walk Away from Omelas

By Ursula Le Guin

With a clamour of bells that set the swallows soaring, the Festival of Summer came to the city of Omelas, bright-towered by the sea. The rigging of the boats in harbor sparkled with flags. In the streets between houses with red roofs and painted walls, between old moss-grown gardens and under avenues of trees, past great parks and public buildings, processions moved. Some were decorous: old people in long stiff robes of mauve and grey, grave master workmen, quiet, merry women carrying their babies and chatting as they walked. In other streets the music beat faster, a shimmering of gong and tambourine, and the people went dancing, the procession was a dance. Children dodged in and out, their high calls rising like the swallows' crossing flights over the music and the singing. All the processions wound towards the north side of the city, where on the great water-meadow called the Green Fields boys and girls, naked in the bright air, with mud-stained feet and ankles and long, lithe arms, exercised their restive horses before the race.

The horses wore no gear at all but a halter without bit. Their manes were braided with streamers of silver, gold and green. They flared their nostrils and pranced and boasted to one another; they were vastly excited, the horse being the only animal who has adopted our ceremonies as his own. Far off to the north and west the mountains stood up half encircling Omelas on her bay.

The air of morning was so clear that the snow still crowning the Eighteen Peaks burned with white-gold fire across the miles of sunlit air, under the dark blue of the sky.

There was just enough wind to make the banners that marked the racecourse snap and flutter now and then. In the silence of the broad green meadows one could hear the music winding through the city streets, farther and nearer and ever approaching, a cheerful faint sweetness of the air that from time to time trembled and gathered together and broke out into the great joyous clanging of the bells. Joyous! How is one to tell about joy? How describe the citizens of Omelas? They were not simple folk, you see, though they were happy. But we do not say the words of cheer much any more. All smiles have become archaic. Given a description such as this one tends to make certain assumptions. Given a description such as this one tends to look next for the King, mounted on a splendid stallion and surrounded by his noble knights, or perhaps in a golden-litter borne by great-muscled slaves. But there was no king. They did not use swords, or keep slaves. They were not barbarians. I do not know the rules and laws of their society, but I suspect that they were singularly few. As they did without monarchy and slavery, so they also got on without the stock exchange, the advertisement, the secret police, and the bomb. Yet I repeat that these were not simple folk, not dulcet shepherds, noble savages, bland utopians. They were not less complex than us.

The trouble is that we have a bad habit, encouraged by pedants and sophisticates, of considering happiness as something rather stupid. Only pain is intellectual, only evil interesting. This is the treason of the artist; a refusal to admit the banality of evil and the terrible boredom of pain. If you can't lick 'em, join 'em. If it hurts, repeat it. But to praise despair is to condemn delight, to embrace violence is to lose hold of everything else. We have almost lost hold; we can no longer describe a happy man, nor make any celebrations of joy. How can I tell you about the people of Omelas?

They were not naive and happy children – though their children were, in fact, happy. They were mature, intelligent, passionate adults whose lives were not wretched. O miracle! but I wish I could describe it better. I wish I could convince you. Omelas sounds in my words like a city in a fairy tale, long ago and far away, once upon a time. Perhaps it would be best if you imagined it as your own fancy bids, assuming it will rise to the occasion, for certainly I cannot suit you all. For instance, how about technology? I think that there would be no cars or helicopters in and above the streets; this follows from the fact that the people of Omelas are happy people. Happiness is based on a just discrimination of what is necessary, what is neither necessary nor destructive, and what is destructive. In the middle category, however – that of the unnecessary but undestructive, that of comfort, luxury, exuberance, etc., etc. – they could perfectly well have central heating, subway trains, washing machines, and all kinds of marvellous devices not yet invented here, floating light-sources, fuelless power, a cure for the common cold. Or they could have none of that; it doesn't matter. As you like it. I incline to think that people from towns up and down the coast have been coming in to Omelas during the last days before the Festival on very fast little trains and double-decked trams, and that the train station of Omelas is actually the handsomest building in town, though plainer than the magnificent Farmers' Market.

But even granted trains, I fear that Omelas so far strikes some of you as goody-goody. Smiles, bells, parades, horses, bleh. If so, please add an orgy. If an orgy would help, don't hesitate. Let us not, however, have temples from which issue beautiful nude priests and priestesses already half in ecstasy and ready to copulate with any man or woman, lover or stranger, who desires union with the deep godhead of the blood, although that was my first idea. But really it would be better not to have any temples in Omelas – at least, not manned temples. Religion yes, clergy no. Surely the beautiful nudes can just wander about offering themselves like divine souffles to the hunger of the needy and the rapture of the flesh. Let them join the processions. Let tambourines be struck above the copulations, and the glory of desire be proclaimed upon the gongs and (a not unimportant point) let the offspring of these delightful rituals be beloved and looked after by all. One thing I know there is none of in Omelas is guilt. But what else should there be? I thought at first there were no drugs, but that is puritanical. For those who like it, the faint insistent sweetness of DROOZ may perfume the ways of the City, DROOZ which first brings a great lightness and brilliance to the mind and limbs, and then after some hours a dreamy languor, and wonderful visions at last of the very arcana and inmost secrets of the Universe, as well as exciting the pleasure of sex beyond all belief; and it is not habit-forming. For more modest tastes I think there ought to be beer. What else, what else belongs in the joyous city? The sense of victory, surely, the celebration of courage. But as we did without clergy, let us do without soldiers. The joy built upon successful slaughter is not the right kind of joy; it will not do, it is fearful and

70

it is trivial. A boundless and generous contentment, a magnanimous triumph felt not against some outer enemy but in communion with the finest and fairest in the souls of all men everywhere and the splendour of the world's summer: this is what swells the hearts of the people of Omelas, and the victory they celebrate is that of life, I really don't think many of them need to take DROOZ.

★ ★ ★

Most of the processions have reached the Green Fields by now. A marvellous smell of cooking goes forth from the red and blue tents of the provisioners. The faces of small children are amiably sticky; in the benign grey beard of a man a couple of crumbs of rich pastry are entangled. The youths and girls have mounted their horses and are beginning to group around the starting line of the course. An old woman, small, fat and laughing, is passing out flowers from a basket, and tall young men wear her flowers in their shining hair. A child of nine or ten sits at the edge of the crowd, alone, playing on a wooden flute. People pause to listen, and they smile, but they do not speak to him for he never ceases playing and never sees them, his dark eyes wholly rapt in the sweet, thin magic of the tune.

He finishes, and slowly lowers his hands holding the wooden flute.

As if that little private silence were the signal, all at once a trumpet sounds from the pavilion near the starting line: imperious, melancholy, piercing. The horses rear on their slender legs, and some of them neigh in answer. Sober-faced, the young riders stroke the horses' necks and soothe them, whispering 'Quiet, quiet, there my beauty, my hope . . . '. They begin to form in rank along the starting line. The crowds along the racecourse are like a field of grass and flowers in the wind. The Festival of Summer has begun.

Do you believe? Do you accept the Festival, the city the joy? No? Then let me describe one more thing.

In a basement under one of the beautiful public buildings of Omelas, or perhaps in the cellar of one of its spacious private homes, there is a room. It has one locked door, and no window. A little light seeps in dustily between cracks in the boards, secondhand from a cobwebbed window somewhere across the cellar. In one corner of the little room a couple of mops, with stiff, clotted, foul-smelling heads, stand near a rusty bucket. The floor is dirt, a little damp to the touch, as cellar dirt usually is. The room is about three paces long and two wide: a mere broom closet or disused tool room. In the room a child is sitting. It could be a boy or a girl. It looks about six, but actually is nearly ten. It is feeble-minded. Perhaps it was born defective, or perhaps it has become imbecile through fear, malnutrition and neglect. It picks its nose and occasionally fumbles vaguely with its toes or genitals, as it sits hunched in the corner farthest from the bucket and two mops. It is afraid of the mops. It finds them horrible. It shuts its eyes, but it knows the mops are still standing there; and the door is locked; and nobody will come. The door is always locked; and nobody ever comes, except that sometimes – the child has no understanding of time or interval – sometimes the door rattles terribly and opens, and a person, or several people, are there. One of them may come in and kick the child to make it stand up. The others never come close, but peer in at it with frightened disgusted eyes. The food bowl and the water jug are hastily filled, the door is locked, the eyes disappear. The people at the door never say anything, but the child, who has not always lived in the tool room and can remember sunlight and its mother's voice, sometimes speaks. 'I will be good' it says. 'Please let me out, I will be good!' They never answer. The child used to scream for help at night, and cry a good deal, but now it only makes a kind of whining, 'eh-haa, eh-haa', and it speaks less and less often. It is so thin there are no calves to its legs; its belly protrudes; it lives on a half-bowl of corn meal and grease a day. It is naked. Its buttocks and thighs are a mass of festered sores, as it sits in its own excrement continually.

They all know it is there, all the people of Omelas. Some of them have come to see it, others are content merely to know it is there. They all know that it has to be there. Some of them understand why, and some do not, but they all understand that their happiness, the beauty of the city, the tenderness of their friendships, the health of their children, the wisdom of their scholars, the skill of their makers, even the abundance of their harvest and the kindly weathers of their skies, depend wholly on this child's abominable misery.

This is usually explained to children when they are between eight and twelve, whenever they seem capable of understanding, and most of those who come to see the child are young people, though often enough an adult comes, or comes back to see the child. No matter how well the matter has been explained to them, these young spectators are always shocked and sickened at the sight. They feel disgust, which they had thought themselves superior to. They feel anger, outrage, impotence, despite all the explanations. They would like to do something for the child. But there is nothing they can do. If the child were brought up into the sunlight out of that vile place, if it were cleaned and fed and comforted, that would be a good thing, indeed; but if it were done, in that day and hour all the prosperity and beauty and delight of Omelas would wither and be destroyed. Those are the terms. To exchange all the goodness and grace of every life in Omelas for that single, small improvement: to throw away all the happiness of thousands for the chance of the happiness of one: that would let guilt within the walls indeed.

The terms are strict and absolute; there may not even be a kind word spoken to the child.

Often the young people go home in tears, or in a tearless rage, when they have seen the child and faced this terrible paradox. They may brood over it for weeks or years. But as time goes on they begin to realise that even if the child could be released, it would not get much good of its freedom: a little vague pleasure of warmth and food, no doubt, but little more. It is too degraded and imbecile to know any real joy. It has been afraid too long ever to be free. Its habits are too uncouth for it to respond to humane treatment. Indeed after so long it would probably be wretched without walls about it to protect it, and darkness for its eyes, and its own excrement to sit in. Their tears at the bitter injustice dry when they begin to perceive the terrible justice of reality and to accept it. Yet it is their tears and anger, the trying of their generosity and the acceptance of their helplessness, which are perhaps the true source of the splendour of their lives. Theirs is no vapid, irresponsible happiness. They know that they, like the child, are not free. They know compassion. It is the existence of the child, and their knowledge of its existence, that makes possible the nobility of their architecture, the poignancy of their music, the profundity of their science. It is because of the child that they are so gentle with children. They know that if the wretched one were not there snivelling in the dark, the other one, the flute-player could make no joyful music as the young riders line up in their beauty for the race in the sunlight of the first morning of summer.

Now do you believe in them? Are they not more credible? But there is one more thing to tell, and this is quite incredible.

At times one of the adolescent girls or boys who go to see the child does not go home to weep or rage, does not, in fact go home at all. Sometimes also a man or woman much older falls silent for a day or two, and then leaves home. These people go out into the street, and walk straight out of the city of Omelas, through the beautiful gates. They keep walking across the farmlands of Omelas. Each one goes alone, youth or girl, man or woman. Night falls; the traveller must pass down the village streets, between the houses with yellow-lit windows, and on out into the darkness of the fields. Each alone, they go west or north, towards the mountains. They go on. They leave Omelas, they walk ahead into the darkness and they do not come back. The place they go towards is a place even less imaginable to most of us than the city of happiness. I cannot describe it at all. It is possible that it does not exist. But they seem to know where they are going, the ones who walk away from Omelas.

(Variations on a theme by William James.)

Private Eloy

By Samuel Feijoo

Eloy was born in the valley of Vega Vieja of peasant parents: his mother a hardworking, smiling mulatto woman, his father a hefty Galician who boasted that he had laid more rails in the region of San Juan de Potreillo than any man on earth. Eloy was the fifth child in the family of nine.

From the time he was very small Eloy knew the land. He was obliged to work hard, from milking-time in the chill of 2 am, when he had to take care of the calves, to the hoeing, the ploughing, the selling of milk in the far-off town. There was not much schooling for Eloy. His mother barely taught him his first letters. His father, an illiterate who could not resign himself to his ignorance, lamented the lack of a school in the valley. Often he would say to his wife, 'If the children could only study a little they could get away from this slavery in the fields. Here they'll throw their lives away working and end up with nothing.'

But no teacher came to the valley of Vega Vieja. Who did come were the Rural Police, the pair of them, riding fat horses, receiving greetings and offerings – a turkey, a couple of chickens – from the intimidated peasants watching the police with ancestral fear. And the peddler of clothes and trinkets, he came, and so did the politician full of smiles and back-slapping, looking for votes and promising projects that never came to anything.

And it was one of these well-dressed, two-faced politicians who, years later, noticed that under his rags

Eloy had the same robust body as his father and proposed to the family, 'If you get me a hundred votes in the Vega Vieja district I'll get him into the army for you . . . But fair's fair. You bring me a hundred pledged votes and I'll fix it with the Colonel.'

This promise fell on Eloy's ears like spring rain on thirsty maize fields. It was irresistible. Although the family had some doubts at first, knowing the politician's lying tongue, they finally came to a decision. 'If he gets into the army the boy's made. Not much work and a pay-packet. Free clothes and food and some money to help us out a bit . . .'

But the prudent Galician was not happy about it. 'If you're a soldier you're the lowest card in the pack. You get kicked around by everyone from the corporal to the lieutenant. He won't study at all, he'll just take orders, no education, nothing and he'll probably end up behaving like all the rest . . .'

But nobody took any notice of him. The family rushed out to look for votes and got promises from half Vega Vieja and even further afield. The result was astounding: more than a hundred pledges. The politician was informed, he collected the list and a few days later he was back with Eloy's papers.

He embraced the young *guajiro*, handed him an envelope and said, 'Fair's fair. Here's your posting. Take this envelope and report to the headquarters in Las Villas.'

And with more embraces all round he went off very pleased with himself, taking the new soldier with him. Eloy was carrying a little bundle containing a change of linen underwear, a pair of socks, a shirt and a spare pair of trousers. He was wearing a *guayabera* of coarse drill, his Sunday best, and thick trousers bagging heavily at the knees in spite of the shiny starch.

At headquarters he was assigned to Santa Clara barracks. There he made friends among the soldiers, peasants like himself, and adapted easily to the discipline of the job. And he felt happy, proud of his khaki uniform and of the arms he carried which gave him a new authority. He had a sense of his importance and enjoyed his position which had rescued him from poverty and toil with no future but a miserable hut and a thankless struggle with the soil.

To begin with he helped his parents with a few pesos and went to visit them in his new uniform, dazzling his family and the neighbours with his rifle and his soldier's trappings, his shiny boots and his complexion, already so much lighter. Eloy was happy.

But his prudent Galician father asked, 'Are you studying?' 'Not yet,' answered his son. 'That's bad. You'll be nothing but a turnip with a tie on. Well-dressed and clean outside and an ignorant clodhopper inside.'

They laughed and said goodbye. And Eloy went back to the city barracks and carried on just the same, without studying, as he couldn't be bothered with reading, and anyway, his life was easy. He knew the value of a peso so he did not waste his money. And he went on helping his parents until he met Eulalia.

His small wages went on her, in presents and taking her out. And one night he carried her off. He rented a room, furnished it sparsely and then Eloy began to feel the pinch. He loved Eulalia and took care that she didn't want for anything.

One afternoon as he was leaving the barracks Lieutenant Valladares said to him, 'You can't go home. We've got an eviction tomorrow in Rio Chiquito.'

Eloy didn't understand what it was all about, but as usual he obeyed. That was the first thing he had been taught, blind obedience to his superiors. He sent a message to Eulalia and resigned himself to the situation.

At dawn they rode out into the countryside. Surrounded by the wildness of nature, the lonely woodland and savannah, with the morning sun shining, the birds singing, the vultures wheeling, the scent of lianas and tender leaves, Eloy felt the joy of his childhood, he was back in his own element. The sun in the open country was doing him good. He rode along cheerfully. He hummed a song.

After six hours' riding they reached Rio Chiquito. There he saw them, at the door of the hut. Their torn clothes, their thin, dry faces, their bare feet, the half-naked children in their arms. Their lifeless eyes. Their silent, pale lips.

The lieutenant said to them, 'You've got to leave. You're being evicted . . .'

The head of the family replied humbly, 'We don't know where to go.' The lieutenant answered, 'We're sorry, we really are sorry. But the law's the law. You've got to get out.' An old man said, 'The law is unjust. We always pay the rent.' The lieutenant replied, 'I've got the legal warrant here – and that's what counts. The land isn't yours and you've got to go. Start loading your stuff onto the cart because we're here to see that the law is carried out.'

Eloy watched the eviction, in silence, disturbed. He saw the thin arms straining to heave the shabby iron beds onto the cart, the wardrobe with two planks missing at the back, the pine table half eaten away by termites, three stools, a cradle with the paint peeling, bundles of clothes, a wooden plough, the stone water-filter, the wash-basin . . . and he thought of his family, thought that the same thing might happen to them.

79

And Eloy was troubled.

They escorted the evicted family to a boundary of coconut palms and after watching them disappear down a lane they went back to the hut and burnt as the lieutenant ordered.

Eloy, holding a flaming branch, his face glowing in the firelight, felt uneasy.

On the way back, as his horse trotted along briskly, nature did not seem so beautiful any more. He felt guilty. He thought of the evicted peasants, of what their fate would be in that countryside where work was non-existent. Facing the rigours of the 'dead season' . . .

When he reached the barracks he felt ill. And that night he found no happiness in Eulalia's arms.

His other disagreeable mission happened during the sugar harvest. There was a strike of workers who were not being paid a fair wage. His detachment arrived in the forecourt of the paralysed refinery. Eloy, together with other soldiers, arrested some workers. He took them out of their houses and made them get into lorries to be taken to the city prisons. He saw them close up, some were peasants like himself. They were justifying themselves, 'We're on strike because they won't give us our rights.' 'Get into the lorry. I don't want any lip from you,' said the lieutenant.

None of the workers put up any resistance against the weapons pointed at them. They climbed into the lorry with an expression of determination. Eloy watched them leave, a twinge of anguish in his heart.

That same day he patrolled around the canefields. Rifle in hand, he walked around the boundaries ready to fire at any striker who might try to set fire to the sugar-cane.

The next day, as he was standing sentinel in the deserted forecourt, a little boy came up to him. 'Guard, mama is ill and needs to go to the doctor. Help me to lift her up. There's no one here. They've all gone.'

Eloy went into the hut and lifted an emaciated woman from the floor. 'She has attacks,' said the child. 'And your father?' asked Eloy. 'He's in prison.' Eloy looked at him uneasily. The unconscious woman sighed faintly. She stretched her limbs and opened her eyes. Eloy quickly asked her. 'Your husband, where is he?' 'He is a striker. He's in prison,' murmured the woman.

Eloy looked at the hut and saw the poverty, the same that he knew so well, the same as in his own hut. He saw the shabby stove with its clay pot, the broken-seated chairs, the beds covered with rags. 'He's in prison,' repeated the little boy.

Eloy was getting fat. He found the life easy. He asked for nothing more. His was a life of simple routine, very different from the heavy labour in the fields where he had had no clean clothes, no good shoes, no money. He would not have changed his status as a soldier for anything in the world. He knew poverty and its despair at close quarters. Nobody was going to make him give up his uniform and his salary. Not even his Eulalia. Nor his two-year-old son. It was a life without ups and downs. Get paid, follow the routine and live . . . No other ideas bothered him much. Politics or injustices or crimes. He was safe. That was how the world was and he had a position in the world, that of a soldier. And that was enough for him. But every now and then he didn't forget the evicted family and the striker's little boy.

In the world around him, not everything was going well for the government. There had been risings in the mountains against the crimes. Despotism was reaping its natural harvest and now the soldiers were going out to fight the rebels in the mountains. The days were not peaceful any more. The war was a bitter reality which he had to face up to. Eloy was not a coward. Eloy knew how to obey. Eloy went to the front.

Eulalia hung religious medals round his neck. She made him accept a charm to ward off bullets, embroidered by her with the Sacred Heart of Jesus in red to protect him from death. She gave him the Prayer of the Just Judge for him to read and carry with him. And Eloy accepted it with a smile. He kissed his son goodbye and held the weeping Eulalia tightly to him.

Eloy knew that the rebels were fighting a bad government. He said to himself, 'All governments are bad and I've got to serve whatever government it happens to be.' And he accepted his position fatalistically. The world was too complicated for him. 'What can I do about it?' he thought.

His lieutenant went with him to the combat zone, leading his detachment. After six exhausting days' marching they reached their objective. 'Let's hope this will soon be over,' said Eloy to his friend Private Julian, a *guajiro* like himself, while the campaign rations were being prepared in a grove of *yagrumas* trees at the foot of a hillside. 'Yes. But it looks a long job . . . Although they haven't a chance against us. Not against the army . . .' Eloy smiled, a little reassured. The breeze blew cool through the leaves of the *yagrumas* which sheltered them.

The mountain peaks looked very near. He could make out the vultures flying, high up, like moving black dots against a Prussian blue firmament. 'Up there,' he said to himself nervously, 'that's where they are.'

At dawn they began the climb. They went forward slowly. An advance party was clearing the way. Behind them marched the main body of soldiers, in single file, well spaced out so as not to make things easy for snipers hidden in the forest. Behind every tree trunk death was spying on them. The weary soldiers were well aware of that.

After five hours' march they pitched camp at the foot of a small hill. One of the first spells of guard duty fell to Private Eloy. He took up his post behind a rock, looking out over a valley full of palm trees and mist. In the distance he could see the sea, a fringe of pale blue. His companion on duty said, 'Not my idea of a good time, stuck here in the bushes.' 'Not mine either. I don't know what we're doing here,' answered Eloy. And they both stared at the horizon, looking for possible signs of rebels.

At nightfall the shooting began. Nobody slept well. Shots that came from nobody knew where. Nervous guards firing. Tense nerves. At first light they continued the weary march, from mountain to mountain through dales and gorges. It was cold and drizzling. A constant mist blurred the trees. Raindrops on the leaves, mud. The soldiers chatted among themselves, 'You can't see a thing.' 'Why aren't we going down yet?' 'Why can't they send somebody else on this wild goose chase?'

At sunrise they came under heavy fire. A group of rebels suddenly blazed away at them. The leading soldiers fell, surprised by bursts of shots coming from no fixed point. Eloy saw them coming back, pale-faced and groaning. The lieutenant, revolver in hand, came up to them. 'Now it's our turn to go ahead. Forward!' And Eloy moved into the vanguard.

A day later he went into battle. As they were going along a path between tall hollyhocks the bullets reached them. Three comrades fell. Eloy fired blindly straight ahead towards the woods. Beside him the machine-guns opened fire on an invisible enemy: the guerrillas. The lieutenant urged them on. 'Into the woods! They're in those woods!'

The soldiers advanced. At full speed. Before reaching the wood ahead several had fallen into the grass. Eloy arrived. He pushed on into the woods. Rifle ready to fire. But he couldn't see anyone. He went on.

From beside the trunk of a *yaba* tree someone spoke to him. It was a bearded man, very young. He was leaning heavily against the tree-trunk, motionless. Eloy went up to him cautiously. He saw the blood. 'I'll take him prisoner,' thought Eloy. He heaved him on to his shoulders. He didn't weigh much. He was a thin man, his uniform torn and dirty. Eloy walked a little way. He got tired. Carefully he laid the wounded man down on the grass while he got his strength back. He listened. There was no sound of shouting any more.

'I'm thirsty. Give me some water.' Eloy pointed his gun at the man's eyes. But all he saw in them was fever and helplessness. 'Water.' Eloy looked at him. It was a peasant face, like his own, a long-suffering face. The wounded man drank from the bottle Eloy handed him. 'Thanks.' 'That's all right,' said Eloy. And he did not know what to do.

'I think I'm badly hurt,' said the wounded man. 'No, no you aren't.' 'I shan't get out of this alive.' Eloy thought, 'If I take this *guajiro* prisoner he'll certainly be murdered. The lieutenant will kill him. He's already killed two *guajiros* just because they couldn't tell him where the rebels were.'

'How old are you?' 'Nineteen,' said the wounded man. Eloy thought, 'If I take him the lieutenant will kill him. I'll leave him here. Let him take his chance. Anyway he can't live long with a Springfield bullet in his stomach.'

The wounded man looked questioningly at him. He could see him thinking. He knew his fate was being decided. 'Come with us, soldier, come on . . . ' Eloy didn't answer. He hesitated. He didn't like the lieutenant and he didn't care for the government. Undecided, he didn't know what to do. 'Come with us,' repeated the young man. 'You carry me and I'll guide you.'

Eloy got up and said, 'I'm going to spare your life, you're a *guajiro* like me. Escape as soon as you can.' 'I can't, soldier, I can't escape. If you go, kill me, I don't want to die here — all by myself. Take me to my people and come and join the revolution.' Eloy said nothing. He turned his back on the wounded man. He walked out of the wood.

'We'd given you up,' said a soldier who was a friend of his. 'They caught us by surprise. There are two dead.'

That night none of the soldiers slept. They were expecting a surprise attack. Eloy, lying awake, thought, 'I'd go, but what about Eulalia and the boy . . . And beginning to face hardships now. When I was all settled in life . . . Poverty in the fields all over again . . . His wound wasn't serious. Wonder if he's still alive? I ought to have killed him really, so he wouldn't suffer any more. But I couldn't have done it.'

At daybreak they were issued with rations. Eloy put aside two bananas, a tin of condensed milk, some biscuits.

And at the first opportunity he slipped away into the woods.

There he was, even paler than before. He was delirious with fever. 'Here, I've brought you some biscuits and bananas and a can of milk . . . ' But the wounded man didn't recognise him. Eloy said to himself, 'If I carry him now I don't know where to take him. Even if I wanted to go with him now he can't guide me . . . '

He found himself surrounded by rifles. The lieutenant shouted, 'Hang them both! Traitors have to be hung!' Eloy saw the ropes, the noose. He didn't try to defend himself.

When the troop turned and looked back for an instant to see if the two bodies had stopped twitching, they saw them swaying in the wind which blew down from the Sierra.

The lieutenant remarked to his shaken orderly, 'I never liked Private Eloy,' he said, scratching his eyebrow. 'He wasn't a safe man.' The orderly said nothing. They crossed a stream, its waters ruffled by the strong breeze. It banks were covered with fine grey sand. The lieutenant knelt down at the water's edge and bathed his eyebrow where a mosquito bite had raised an irritating swelling.

The Assignment

By Saadat Hasan Manto
(Translated from the Urdu)

Beginning with isolated incidents of stabbing, it had now developed into full-scale communal violence, with no holds barred. Even home-made bombs were being used.

The general view in Amritsar was that the riots could not last long. They were seen as no more than a manifestation of temporarily inflamed political passions which were bound to cool down before long. After all, these were not the first communal riots the city had known. There had been so many of them in the past. They never lasted long. The pattern was familiar. Two weeks or so of unrest and then business as usual. On the basis of experience, therefore, the people were quite justified in believing that the current troubles would also run their course in a few days. But this did not happen. They not only continued, but grew in intensity.

Muslims living in Hindu localities began to leave for safer places, and Hindus in Muslim majority areas followed suit. However, everyone saw these adjustments as strictly temporary. The atmosphere would soon be clear of this communal madness, they told themselves.

Retired judge Mian Adbul Hai was absolutely confident that things would return to normal soon, which was why he wasn't worried. He had two children, a boy of eleven and a girl of seventeen. In addition, there was an old servant who was now pushing seventy. It was a

87

small family. When the troubles started, Mian *sahib**, being an extra cautious man, stocked up on food . . . just in case. So on one count, at least, there were no worries.

His daughter Sughra was less sure of things. They lived in a three-storey house with a view over almost the entire city. Sughra could not help noticing that whenever she went on the roof, there were fires raging everywhere. In the beginning, she could hear fire engines rushing past, their bells ringing, but this had now stopped. There were too many fires in too many places.

The nights had become particularly frightening. The sky was always lit by conflagrations like giants spitting out flames. Then there were the slogans which rent the air with terrifying frequency – Allaho Akbar, Har Har Mahadev.

Sughra never expressed her fears to her father, because he had declared confidently that there was no cause for anxiety. Everything was going to be fine. Since he was generally always right, she had initially felt reassured.

However, when the power and water supplies were suddenly cut off, she expressed her unease to her father and suggested apologetically that, for a few days at least, they should move to Sharifpura, a Muslim locality, to where many of the old residents had already moved. Mian sahib was adamant: 'You're imagining things. Everything is going to be normal very soon.'

He was wrong. Things went from bad to worse. Before long there was not a single Muslim family to be found in Mian Abdul Hai's locality. Then one day Mian sahib suffered a stroke and was laid up. His son Basharat, who

*sahib: sir, master

used to spend most of his time playing self-devised games, now stayed glued to his father's bed.

All the shops in the area had been permanently boarded up. Dr Ghulam Hussain's dispensary had been shut for weeks and Sughra had noticed from the roof-top one day that the adjoining clinic of Dr Goranditta Mall was also closed. Mian sahib's condition was getting worse day by day. Sughra was almost at the end of her wits. One day she took Basharat aside and said to him, 'You've got to do something. I know it's not safe to go out, but we must get some help. Our father is very ill.'

The boy went, but came back almost immediately. His face was pale with fear. He had seen a blood-drenched body lying in the street and a group of wild-looking men looting shops. Sughra took the terrified boy in her arms and said a silent prayer, thanking God for his safe return. However, she could not bear her father's suffering. His left side was now completely lifeless. His speech had been impaired and he mostly communicated through gestures, all designed to reassure Sughra that soon all would be well.

It was the month of Ramadan and only two days to Id*. Mian sahib was quite confident that the troubles would be over by then. He was again wrong. A canopy of smoke hung over the city, with fires burning everywhere. At night the silence was shattered by deafening explosions. Sughra and Basharat hadn't slept for days.

Sughra, in any case, couldn't because of her father's deteriorating condition. Helplessly, she would look at him, then at her young frightened brother and the seventy-year-old servant Akbar, who was useless for all

*Id: a muslim festival

practical purposes. He mostly kept to his bed, coughing and fighting for breath. One day Sughra told him angrily, 'What good are you? Do you realise how ill Mian sahib is? Perhaps you are too lazy to want to help, pretending that you are suffering from acute asthma. There was a time when servants used to sacrifice their lives for their masters.'

Sughra felt very bad afterwards. She had been unnecessarily harsh on the old man. In the evening when she took his food to him in his small room, he was not there. Basharat looked for him all over the house but he was nowhere to be found. The front door was unlatched. He was gone, perhaps to get some help for Mian sahib. Sughra prayed for his return, but two days passed and he hadn't come back.

It was evening and the festival of Id was now only a day away. She remembered the excitement which used to grip the family on this occasion. She remembered standing on the roof-top, peering into the sky, looking for the Id moon and praying for the clouds to clear. But how different everything was today. The sky was covered in smoke and on distant roofs one could see people looking upwards. Were they trying to catch sight of the new moon or were they watching the fires, she wondered?

She looked up and saw the thin sliver of the moon peeping through a small patch in the sky. She raised her hands in prayer, begging God to make her father well. Basharat, however, was upset that there would be no Id this year.

The night hadn't yet fallen. Sughra had moved her father's bed out of the room onto the veranda. She was sprinkling water on the floor to make it cool. Mian sahib was lying there quietly looking with vacant eyes at the sky where she had seen the moon. Sughra came and sat next to him. He motioned her to get closer. Then he raised his right arm slowly and put it on her head. Tears began to run from Sughra's eyes. Even Mian sahib looked moved. Then with great difficulty he said to her, 'God is merciful. All will be well.'

Suddenly there was a knock on the door. Sughra's heart began to beat violently. She looked at Basharat, whose face had turned white like a sheet of paper. There was another knock. Mian sahib gestured to Sughra to answer it. It must be old Akbar who had come back, she thought. She said to Basharat, 'Answer the door. I'm sure it's Akbar.' Her father shook his head, as if to signal disagreement.

'Then who can it be?' Sughra asked him.

Mian Abdul Hai tried to speak, but before he could do so, Basharat came running in. He was breathless. Taking Sughra aside, he whispered, 'It's a Sikh.'

Sughra screamed, 'A Sikh! What does he want?'

'He wants me to open the door.'

Sughra took Basharat in her arms and went and sat on her father's bed, looking at him desolately.

On Mian Abdul Hai's thin, lifeless lips, a faint smile appeared. 'Go and open the door. It is Gurmukh Singh.'

'No, it's someone else,' Basharat said.

Mian sahib turned to Sughra. 'Open the door. It's him.'

Sughra rose. She knew Gurmukh Singh. Her father had once done him a favour. He had been involved in a false legal suit and Mian sahib had acquitted him. That was a long time ago, but every year on the occasion of Id, he would come all the way from his village with a bag of home-made noodles. Mian sahib had told him several times, 'Sardar sahib, you really are too kind.

You shouldn't inconvenience yourself every year.' But Gurmukh Singh would always reply, 'Mian sahib, God has given you everything. This is only a small gift which I bring every year in humble acknowledgement of the kindness you did me once. Even a hundred generations of mine would not be able to repay your favour. May God keep you happy.'

Sughra was reassured. Why hadn't she thought of it in the first place? But why had Basharat said it was someone else? After all, he knew Gurmukh Singh's face from his annual visit.

Sughra went to the front door. There was another knock. Her heart missed a beat. 'Who is it?' she asked in a faint voice.

Basharat whispered to her to look through a small hole in the door.

It wasn't Gurmukh Singh, who was a very old man. This was a young fellow. He knocked again. He was holding a bag in his hand, of the same kind Gurmukh Singh used to bring.

'Who are you?' she asked, a little more confident now.

'I am Sardar Gurmukh Singh's son Santokh.'

Sughra's fear had suddenly gone. 'What brings you here today?' she asked politely.

'Where is judge sahib?' he asked.

'He is not well,' Sughra answered.

'Oh, I'm sorry,' Santokh Singh said. Then he shifted his bag from one hand to the other. 'These are home-made noodles.' Then after a pause, '*Sardarji** is dead.'

'Dead!'

***Sardarji**: a respectful way to address a Sikh man

'Yes, a month ago, but one of the last things he said to me was, "For the last ten years, on the occasion of Id, I have always taken my small gift to judge sahib. After I am gone, it will become your duty." I gave him my word that I would not fail him. I am here today to honour the promise made to my father on his death-bed.'

Sughra was so moved that tears came to her eyes. She opened the door a little. The young man pushed the bag towards her. 'May God rest his soul,' she said.

'Is judge sahib not well?' he asked.

'No.'

'What's wrong?'

'He had a stroke.'

'Had my father been alive, it would have grieved him deeply. He never forgot judge sahib's kindness until his last breath. He used to say, "He is not a man, but a god." May God keep him under his care. Please convey my respects to him.'

He left before Sughra could make up her mind whether or not to ask him to get a doctor.

As Santokh Singh turned the corner, four men, their faces covered with their turbans, moved towards him. Two of them held burning oil torches, the others carried cans of kerosene oil and explosives. One of them asked Santokh, 'Sardar Ji, have you completed your assignment?'

The young man nodded.

'Should we then proceed with ours?' he asked.

'If you like,' he replied and walked away.

Rules of the Game

By Amy Tan

I was six when my mother taught me the art of invisible strength. It was a strategy for winning arguments, respect from others, and eventually, though neither of us knew it at the time, chess games.

'Bite back your tongue,' scolded my mother when I cried loudly, yanking her hand toward a store that sold bags of salted plums. At home, she said, 'Wise guy, he not go against the wind. In Chinese we say, Come from South, blow with wind – poom! – North will follow. Strongest wind cannot be seen.'

The next week I bit back my tongue as we entered the store with the forbidden candles. When my mother finished her shopping, she quietly plucked a small bag of salted plums from the rack and put it on the counter with the rest of the items.

★ ★ ★

My mother imparted her daily truths so she could help my older brothers and me rise above our circumstances. We lived in San Francisco's Chinatown. Like most of the other Chinese children who played in the back alleys of restaurants and curio shops, I didn't think we were poor. My bowl was always full, three five-course meals every day, beginning with a soup full of mysterious things I didn't want to know the names of.

We lived on Waverly Place, in a warm, clean two-bedroom flat that sat above a small Chinese bakery specializing in steam pastries and dim sum. In the early morning, when the alley was still quiet, I could smell fragrant red beans as they were cooked down to a pasty sweetness. By daybreak, our flat was heavy with the odor of fried sesame balls and sweet curried chicken crescents. From my bed, I would listen as my father got ready for work, then locked the door behind him, one–two–three clicks.

At the end of our two–block alley was a small sandlot playground with swings and slides well-shined down the middle with use. The play area was bordered by wood-slat benches where old-country people sat cracking roasted watermelon seeds with their golden teeth and scattering the husks to an impatient gathering of gurgling pigeons. The best playground, however, was the dark alley itself. It was crammed with daily mysteries and adventures. My brothers and I would peer into the medicinal herb shop, watching old Li dole out onto a stiff sheet of white paper the right amount of insect shells, saffron-colored seeds and pungent leaves for his ailing customers. It was said that he once cured a woman of dying of an ancestral curse that had eluded the best of American doctors. Next to the pharmacy was a printer who specialized in gold-embossed wedding invitations and festive red banners.

Farther down the street was Ping Yuen Fish Market. The front window displayed a tank crowded with doomed fish and turtles struggling to gain footing on the slimy green-tiled sides. A hand-written sign informed tourists, 'Within this store, is all for food, not for pet.' Inside, the butchers with their bloodstained white smocks deftly guttered the fish while customers cried out their orders and shouted, 'Give me your freshest.' On less crowded market days, we would inspect the crates of live frogs and crabs which we were warned not to poke, boxes of dried cuttlefish, and row upon row of iced prawns, squid and slippery fish. The sanddabs made me shiver each time; their eyes lay on one flattened side and reminded me of my mother's story of a careless girl who ran into a crowded street and was crushed by a cab. 'Was smash flat,' reported my mother.

At the corner of the alley was Hong Sing's, a four-table café with a recessed stairwell in front that led to a door marked 'Tradesmen'. My brothers and I believed the bad people emerged from this door at night. Tourists never went to Hong Sing's, since the menu was printed only in Chinese. A Caucasian man with a big camera once posed me and my playmates in front of the restaurant. He had us move to the side of the picture window so the photo would capture the roasted duck with its head dangling from a juice-covered rope. After he took the picture, I told him he should go into Hong Sing's and eat dinner. When he smiled and asked me what they served, I shouted, 'Guts and duck's feet and octopus gizzards!' Then I ran off with my friends, shrieking with laughter as we scampered across the alley and hid in the entryway grotto of the China Gem Company, my heart pounding with hope that he would chase us.

My mother named me after the street that we lived on: Waverley Place Jong, my official name for important American documents. But my family called me Meimei, 'Little Sister'. I was the youngest, the only daughter. Each morning before school, my mother would twist and yank on my thick black hair until she had formed two tightly wound pigtails. One day, as she struggled to weave a hard-toothed comb through my disobedient hair, I had a sly thought.

I asked her, 'Ma, what is Chinese torture?' My mother shook her head. A bobby pin was wedged between her lips. She wetted her palm and smoothed the hair above my ear, then pushed the pin in so that it nicked sharply against my scalp.

'Who say this word?' she asked without a trace of knowing how wicked I was being. I shrugged my shoulders and said, 'Some boy in my class said Chinese people do Chinese torture.'

'Chinese people do many things,' she said simply. 'Chinese people do business, do medicine, do painting. Not lazy like American people. We do torture. Best torture.'

★ ★ ★

My older brother Vincent was the one who actually got the chess set. We had gone to the annual Christmas party held at the First Chinese Baptist Church at the end of the alley. The missionary ladies had put together a Santa bag of gifts donated by members of another church. None of the gifts had names on them. There were separate sacks for boys and girls of different ages.

One of the Chinese parishioners had donated a Santa Claus costume and a stiff paper beard with cotton balls glued to it. I think the only children who thought he were the real thing were too young to know that Santa Claus was not Chinese. When my turn came up, the Santa man asked me how old I was. I thought it was a trick question; I was seven according to the American formula and eight by the Chinese calendar. I said I was born on March 17, 1951. That seemed to satisfy him. He then solemnly asked if I had been a very, very good girl this year and did I believe in Jesus Christ and obey my parents. I knew the only answer to that. I nodded back with equal solemnity.

Having watched the other children opening their gifts, I already knew that the big gifts were not necessarily the nicest ones. One girl my age got a large coloring book of biblical characters, while a less greedy girl who selected a smaller box received a glass vial of lavender toilet water. The sound of a box was also important. A ten-year-old boy had chosen a box that jangled when he shook it. It was a tin globe of the world with a slit for inserting money. He must have thought it was full of dimes and nickels, because when he saw that it had just ten pennies, his face fell with such undisguised disappointment that his mother slapped the side of his head and led him out of the church hall, apologizing to the crowd for her son who had such bad manners he couldn't appreciate such a fine gift.

As I peered into the sack, I quickly fingered the remaining presents, testing their weight, imagining what they contained. I chose a heavy, compact one that was wrapped in shiny silver foil and a red satin ribbon. It was a twelve-pack of Life Savers and I spent the rest of the party arranging and rearranging the candy tubes in the order of my favourites. My brother Winston chose wisely as well. His present turned out to be a box of intricate plastic parts; the instructions on the box proclaimed that when they were properly assembled he would have an authentic miniature replica of a World War II submarine.

Vincent got the chess set, which would have been a very decent present to get at a church Christmas party, except it was obviously used and, as we discovered later, it was missing a black pawn and a white knight. My mother graciously thanked the unknown benefactor, saying, 'Too good. Cost too much.' At which point, an old lady with fine white, wispy hair nodded toward our family and said with a whistling whisper, 'Merry, merry Christmas.'

When we got home, my mother told Vincent to throw the chess set away. 'She not want it. We not want it,' she said, tossing her head stiffly to the side with a tight, proud smile. My brothers had deaf ears. They were already lining up the chess pieces and reading from the dog-eared instruction book.

* * *

I watched Vincent and Winston play during Christmas week. The chessboard seemed to hold elaborate secrets waiting to be untangled. The chessmen were more powerful than old Li's magic herbs that cured ancestral curses. And my brothers wore such serious faces that I was sure something was at stake that was greater than avoiding the tradesmen's door to Hong Sing's.

'Let me! Let me!' I begged between games when one brother or the other would sit back with a deep sigh of relief and victory, the other annoyed, unable to let go of the outcome. Vincent at first refused to let me play, but when I offered my Life Savers as replacements for the buttons that filled in for the missing pieces, he relented. He chose the flavours: wild cherry for the black pawn and peppermint for the white knight. Winner could eat both.

As our mother sprinkled flour and rolled out small doughy circles for the steamed dumplings that would be our dinner that night, Vincent explained the rules, pointing to each piece: 'You have sixteen pieces and so do I. One king and queen, two bishops, two knights, two castles and eight pawns. The pawns can only move forward one step, except on the first move. Then they can move two. But they can only take men by moving crossways like this, except in the beginning, when you can move ahead and take another pawn.

'Why?' I asked as I moved my pawn. 'Why can't they move more steps?'

'Because they're pawns,' he said.

'But why do they go crossways to take other men? Why aren't there any women and children?'

'Why is the sky blue? Why must you always ask stupid questions?' asked Vincent. 'This is a game. These are the rules. I didn't make them up. See. Here. In the book.' He jabbed a page with a pawn in his hand. 'Pawn. P-A-W-N. Pawn. Read it yourself.'

My mother patted the flour off her hands. 'Let me see book,' she said quietly. She scanned the pages quickly, not reading the foreign symbols, seeming to search deliberately for nothing in particular.

'This American rules,' she concluded at last. 'Every time people come out from a foreign country, must know rules. You not know, judge say, Too bad, go back. They not telling you why so you can use their way go forward. They say, Don't know why, you find out yourself. But they knowing all the time. Better you take it, find out why yourself.' She tossed her head back with a satisfied smile.

I found out about all the whys later. I read the rules and looked up the big words in a dictionary. I borrowed books from the China-town library. I studied each chess piece, trying to absorb the power each contained.

I learned about opening moves and why it's important to control the centre early on; the shortest distance between two points is straight down the middle. I learned about the middle game and why tactics between two adversaries are like clashing ideas; the one who plays better has the clearest plans for both attacking and getting out of traps. I learned why it is essential in the endgame to have foresight, a mathematical understanding of all possible moves, and patience; all weaknesses and advantages become evident to a strong adversary and are obscured to a tiring opponent. I discovered that for the whole game one must gather invisible strengths and see the endgame before the game begins.

I also found out why I should never reveal 'why' to others. A little knowledge withheld is a great advantage one should store for future use. That is the power of chess. It is a game of secrets in which one must show but never tell.

I loved the secrets I found within the sixty-four black and white squares. I carefully drew a handmade chessboard and pinned it to the wall next to my bed, where at night I would stare for hours at imaginary battles. Soon I no longer lost any games or Life Savers, but I lost my adversaries. Winston and Vincent decided they were more interested in roaming the streets after school in their Hopalong Cassidy cowboy hats.

★ ★ ★

On a cold spring afternoon, while walking home from school, I detoured through the playground at the end of our alley. I saw a group of old men, two seated across a folding table playing a game of chess, others smoking

101

pipes, eating peanuts and watching. I ran home and grabbed Vincent's chess set, which was bound in a cardboard box with rubber bands. I also carefully selected two prized rolls of Life Savers. I came back to the park and approached a man who was observing the game.

'Want to play?' I asked him. His face widened with surprise and he grinned as he looked at the box under my arm.

'Little sister, been a long time since I play with dolls,' he said, smiling benevolently. I quickly put the box down next to him on the bench and displayed my retort.

Lau Po, as he allowed me to call him, turned out to be a much better player than my brothers. I lost many games and many Life Savers. But over the weeks, with each diminishing roll of candies, I added new secrets. Lau Po gave me the names. The Double Attack from the East and West Shores. Throwing Stones on the Drowning Man. The Sudden Meeting of the Clan. The Surprise from the Sleeping Guard. The Humble Servant Who Kills the King. Sand in the Eyes of Advancing Forces. A Double Killing Without Blood.

There were also the fine points of chess etiquette. Keep captured men in neat rows, as well-tended prisoners. Never announce 'Check' with vanity, lest someone with an unseen sword slit your throat. Never hurl pieces into the sandbox after you have lost a game, because then you must find them again, by yourself, after apologizing to all around you. By the end of summer, Lau Po had taught me all he knew, and I had become a better chess player.

A small weekend crowd of Chinese people and tourists would gather as I played and defeated my opponents one by one. My mother would join the crowds during these outdoor exhibition games. She sat proudly on the bench, telling my admirers with proper Chinese humility, 'Is luck.'

A man who watched me play in the park suggested that my mother allow me to play in local chess tournaments. My mother smiled graciously, an answer that meant nothing. I desperately wanted to go, but bit back my tongue. I knew she would not let me play among strangers. So as we walked home I said in a small voice that I didn't want to play in the local tournament. They would have American rules. If I lost, I would bring shame on my family.

'Is shame you fall down nobody push you,' said my mother.

During my first tournament, my mother sat with me in the front row as I waited for my turn. I frequently bounced my legs to unstick them from the cold metal seat of the folding chair. When my name was called, I leapt up. My mother unwrapped something in her lap. It was her *chang*, a small tablet of red jade which held the sun's fire. 'Is luck,' she whispered and tucked it into my dress pocket. I turned to my opponent, a fifteen-year-old boy from Oakland. He looked at me, wrinkling his nose.

As I began to play, the boy disappeared, the color ran out of the room and I saw only my white pieces and his black ones waiting on the other side. A light wind began blowing past my ears. It whispered secrets only I could hear.

'Blow from the South,' it murmured. 'The wind leaves no trail.' I saw a clear path, the traps to avoid. The crowd rustled. 'Shhh! Shhh!' said the corners of the room. The wind blew stronger. 'Throw sand from the East to distract him.' The knight came forward ready for the sacrifice. The wind hissed, louder and louder. 'Blow, blow, blow. He cannot see. He is blind now. Make him lean away from the wind so he is easier to knock down.'

'Check,' I said, as the wind roared with laughter. The wind died down to little puffs, my own breath.

My mother placed my first trophy next to a new plastic chess set that the neighbourhood Tao society had given to me. As she wiped each piece with a soft cloth, she said, 'Next time win more, lose less.'

'Ma, it's not how many pieces you lose,' I said. 'Sometimes you need to lose pieces to get ahead.'

'Better to lose less, see if you really need.'

At the next tournament, I won again, but it was my mother who wore the triumphant grin.

'Lost eight piece this time. Last time was eleven. What I tell you? Better off lose less!' I was annoyed, but I couldn't say anything.

I attended more tournaments, each one farther away from home. I won all games, in all divisions. The Chinese bakery downstairs from our flat displayed my growing collection of trophies in its window, amidst the dust-covered cakes that were never picked up. The day after I won an important regional tournament, the window encased a fresh sheet cake with whipped-cream frosting and red script saying 'Congratulations, Waverly Jong, Chinatown Chess Champion.' Soon after that, a flower shop, headstone engraver and funeral parlor offered to sponsor me in national tournaments. That's when my mother decided I no longer had to do the dishes. Winston and Vincent had to do my chores.

'Why does she get to play and we do all the work?' complained Vincent.

'Is new American rules,' said my mother. 'Meimei play, squeeze all her brains out for win chess. You play, worth squeeze towel.'

By my ninth birthday, I was a national chess champion. I was still some 429 points away from grand-master status, but I was touted as the Great American Hope, a child prodigy and a girl to boot. They ran a photo of me in *Life* magazine next to a quote in which Bobby Fischer said, 'There will never be a woman grand master. 'Your Move, Bobby,' said the caption.

The day they took the magazine picture I wore neatly plaited braids clipped with plastic barrettes trimmed with rhinestones. I was playing in a large high school auditorium that echoed with phlegmy coughs and the squeaky rubber knobs of chair legs sliding across freshly waxed wooden floors. Seated across from me was an American man, about the same age as Lau Po, maybe fifty. I remember that his sweaty brow seemed to weep at my every move. He wore a dark, malodorous suit. One of his pockets was stuffed with a great white kerchief on which he wiped his palm before sweeping his hand over the chosen chess piece with great flourish.

In my crisp pink-and-white dress with scratchy lace at the neck, one of two my mother had sewn for these special occasions, I would clasp my hands under my chin, the delicate points of my elbows poised lightly on the table in the manner my mother had shown me for posing for the press. I would swing my patent leather shoes back and forth like an impatient child riding on a school bus. Then I would pause, suck in my lips, twirl my chosen piece in midair as if undecided, and then firmly plant it in its new threatening place, with a triumphant smile thrown back at my opponent for good measure.

★ ★ ★

I no longer played in the alley of Waverly Place. I never visited the playground where the pigeons and old men gathered, I went to school, then directly home to learn new chess secrets, cleverly concealed advantages, more escape routes.

But I found it difficult to concentrate at home. My mother had a habit of standing over me while I plotted out my games. I think she thought of herself as my protective ally. Her lips would be sealed tight, and after each move I made, a soft 'Hmmmmph' would escape from her nose.

'Ma, I can't practise when you stand there like that,' I said one day. She retreated to the kitchen and made loud noises with the pots and pans. When the crashing stopped I could see out of the corner of my eye that she was standing in the doorway. 'Hmmmph!' Only this one came out of her tight throat.

My parents made many concessions to allow me to practise. One time I complained that the bedroom I shared was so noisy that I couldn't think. Thereafter, my brothers slept in a bed in the living room facing the street. I said I couldn't finish my rice; my head didn't work right when my stomach was too full. I left the table with half-finished bowls and nobody complained. But there was one duty I couldn't avoid. I had to accompany my mother on Saturday market days when I had no tournament to play. My mother would proudly walk with me, visiting many shops, buying very little. 'This is my daughter Wave-ly Jong,' she said to whoever looked her way.

One day after we left a shop I said under my breath, 'I wish you wouldn't do that, telling everybody I'm your daughter.' My mother stopped walking. Crowds of people with heavy bags pushed past us on the sidewalk, bumping into first one shoulder, then another.

'Aiii-ya. So shame be with mother?' She grasped my hand even tighter as she glared at me.

I looked down. 'It's not that, it's just so obvious. It's just so embarrassing.'

'Embarrass you be my daughter?' Her voice was cracking with anger.

'That's not what I meant. That's not what I said.'

'What you say?'

I knew it was a mistake to say anything more, but I heard my voice speaking, 'Why do you have to use me to show off? If you want to show off, then why don't you learn to play chess?'

My mother's eyes turned into dangerous black slits. She had no words for me, just sharp silence.

I felt the wind rushing around my hot ears. I jerked my mother's tight grasp and spun around, knocking into an old woman. Her bag of groceries spilled to the ground.

'Aii-ya! Stupid girl!' my mother and the woman cried. Oranges and tin cans careened down the sidewalk. As my mother stooped to help the old woman pick up the escaping food, I took off.

I raced down the street, dashing between people, not looking back as my mother screamed shrilly, 'Meimei! Meimei!' I fled down an alley, past dark, curtained shops and merchants washing the grime off their windows. I sped into the sunlight, into a large street crowded with tourists examining trinkets and souvenirs. I ducked into another dark alley, down another street, up another alley. I ran until it hurt and I realized I had nowhere to go, that I was not running from anything. The alleys contained no escape routes.

My breath came out like angry smoke. It was cold. I sat down on an upturned plastic pail next to a stack of empty boxes, cupping my chin with my hands, thinking hard. I imagined my mother, first walking briskly down one street or another looking for me, then giving up and returning home to await my arrival. After two hours, I stood up on creaking legs and slowly walked home.

The alley was quiet and I could see the yellow lights shining from our flat like two tiger's eyes in the night. I climbed the sixteen steps to the door, advancing quietly up each so as not to make any warning sounds. I turned the knob; the door was locked. I heard a chair moving, quick steps, the locks turning – click! click! click! – and then the door opened.

'About time you got home,' said Vincent. 'Boy, are you in trouble.'

He slid back to the dinner table. On a platter were the remains of a large fish, its fleshy head still connected to bones swimming upstream in vain escape. Standing there waiting my punishment, I heard my mother speak in a dry voice.

'We not concerning this girl. This girl not have concerning for us.'

Nobody looked at me. Bone chopsticks clinked against the inside of bowls being emptied into hungry mouths.

I walked into my room, closed the door, and lay down on my bed. The room was dark, the ceiling filled with shadows from the dinnertime lights of neighbouring flats.

In my head, I saw a chessboard with sixty-four black and white squares. Opposite me was my opponent, two angry black slits. She wore a triumphant smile. 'Strongest wind cannot be seen,' she said.

Her black men advanced across the plane, slowly marching to each successive level as a single unit. My white pieces screamed as they scurried and fell off the board one by one. As her men drew closer to my edge, I felt myself growing light. I rose up into the air and flew out the window. Higher and higher, above the alley, over the tops of tiled roofs, where I was gathered up by the wind and pushed up toward the night sky until everything below me disappeared and I was alone.

I closed my eyes and pondered my next move.

Tightrope

By Romesh Gunesekera

[1]

'Oscar! Come and eat.'

My mother's voice was always sharp. The words snagged on the net curtains hung out to dry on the landing. I ignored them. They were old words. I'd heard them before. Every day for as long as I could remember. They were the sounds of time passing: like the buses on the road, or water in the pipes, the whine of a washing machine stuck in a rut.

'Oscar, *food.*'

She and Lenny, my younger brother, would be picking at chicken bones, leftover rice, curried vegetables that had been crushed into one another; eating loudly and clucking from the kitchen to the back extension until they lost the point of it all. Even on a Sunday that my father was at home, it was not much different. They'd congregate in one place then, but still munch mindlessly to themselves and get lost in shopping lists, lottery grunts or yesterday's junk mail. Farmyard feeders in suburban gear, that's what they were.

I picked up the remote and pressed the red button. The screen in the corner flared with a zing and I felt sucked in. Rubbery. I liked that. But the face on the screen, I didn't like. With my thumb I pressed the channel-up button several times, then held it down like an accelerator and watched half a dozen screen faces flash by. I liked that too. The idea that there were so many out

110

there which I could ignore: turn off. Not you, not you, not you.

'Oscar, if you're not eating I'll put the rice in the fridge. You take what you want. I have to go in ten minutes to drop Lenny.'

Thank you, I replied politely in my mind. You don't have to say it long as you've thought it. I didn't want food just then. My hunger was for something more . . . *intangible*, like fleeting images that disappeared – phantom fish in a pool, suggesting possibilities but never becoming solid, heavy, cooked and dead.

'Oscar? You must eat something. And remember, we go back to the hospital at six. Be ready.'

'OK.'

I bit my lip too late. The OK had slipped out. It always makes me cross to realize I have so little control. The one word hung in the room, accusing me of a weak will. A loose mouth. Two syllables. Two silly bells. My father would not have given in so easily. But then I pictured him sunk in his hospital bed, giving in. I quickly pressed the remote again. The TV blinked. A grey ghost faded, wordlessly, into the screen.

[2]

Sparrow told me the other day that willpower was what made humans human. 'No willpower, no nothing.'

I'd never considered that. We were in my room, thinking. Recently we'd both discovered how wild this could be.

'Think about it. If you have no will, you live like a dog. You just react.'

111

'But *you* react. You react all the time.' I was not going to just sit back and swallow any old tripe he threw up in the air. No way.

Sparrow screwed up his face until his lips and eyes disappeared into thin folds of skin. His puckered head shifted back and relocated in the depths of his shoulders. He had no neck left. 'That's cos I want to react. If I didn't want to, I could hold back. No react or react – it's my choice. That's willpower. Real power.'

'Anyway, a dog knows stuff too. They choose too.' I wasn't very happy with his line of discrimination. I like dogs. A dog's life, I think, could be paradise. Wordless. Real. Imagine what you would see as a dog. Everything would be from a lower altitude. Lower even than Lenny. Everything big would be taller and longer. Wilder and weirder.

Sparrow claimed that dogs don't even see in colour, but how would he know? How would anyone but a dog really know? Anyway, maybe they smell and hear colour instead. They remember things – so, what lights up in their heads then? What would my red socks be like? Rina's blue-glass bangles? Imagine taste instead of colour. Texture. Sound. It could be OK, as a life.

Sparrow pulled his legs into a lotus position, withdrawing.

'So, what are you doing now?' I asked. I had learned to be wary with him.

'Waiting.'

'For what?'

'The right time.'

Now that, I thought, was something neat. I was also waiting for the right time. But until Sparrow said it, I had never realized it. I hadn't thought that I too could be waiting for a sense of willpower to grow in me and tell me what to do. Tell me what I wanted, besides the obvious stuff that everybody wanted. Or said they wanted.

Sparrow talked rubbish most of the time, but there was something in what he said about willpower and waiting that stuck, like a string of celery between my teeth. It made me think about Sparrow in a different way. Sometimes he said exactly the words you needed, almost by accident. Come to think of it, he was a celery stick himself. Especially with his shabby cords and wilted hair.

Sparrow said he had deep lines, like crevices, running down the soles of his feet. 'You have lines like that?' he asked slyly.

'I dunno,' I said.

'Let's see.'

'I don't want you looking at my feet.'

'They tell the future, you know, those lines.'

'That's on your palm, you idiot.' I was not going to be tricked so easily.

'This is something else. A special thing my sister taught me.'

Sparrow's sister was clever. She carried a lot of knowledge, easily. I was often damaged just by the thought of her.

'You can read them?'

Sparrow nodded.

'OK then,' I said, and peeled off my socks. There were things I wanted to know. About myself. The past. The future. Sparrow's big sister. I was in that kind of a mood.

Sparrow peered forward and made a sound with his tongue like something was gurgling down a plughole. 'Too faint. Those are way too faint.'

113

I twisted my foot upwards to check for myself.
I could make out a few spidery wrinkles but most of the
skin looked like melted candle wax. Some patches were
speckled with black grime and glossed over like a dirty
gym floor. The arch of the foot seemed very pale and
seriously deformed.

'You have to rub lemon juice for those lines to really
show up.'

'Rubbish.'

Sparrow shrugged.

I hobbled over to the bathroom to wash my feet
instead. While I was rinsing them in the bath, Sparrow
shouted out that he had to go. He left.

When I returned I couldn't find my socks anywhere.
I didn't mind at first. It's not unusual not to be able to
find things in here. The universe, they say, is a mystery.
So's my room. I had no reason to suspect anything.

[3]

On Channel Four, a goldfish was pumping hard, the heart
beating ultra-fast. It looked like it couldn't go on much
longer. I used my thumb for the mute button. I had read
in *The Book of Deeper Secrets* that every heart has a number.
A number of beats it will beat no matter what. Nothing
can stop the number; nothing can extend it. You could
cross a desert without water if you hadn't reached the
last number. You could swim the Atlantic, underwater, if
you had enough beats. Basically, you survive anything if you
are meant to. I liked the idea. So very sub-zero.

My father, propped up in his sickbed, was not
impressed when I mentioned what I'd discovered.
He said that such stories were dangerous nonsense. The

114

heart is an organ, not a clock. He broke the word to emphasize it. *Ker-lock.* 'You don't wind it up.'

But hey, Dad, hello? Nobody winds clocks any more.

[4]

TV muted, I rolled over to the window. Years of moisture had collected on the lower edges making them sag and turn black with mildew. Outside, the sky looked as if it was made of metal. The clouds were low enough to suck, like stage-smoke. A few autumn crocuses spiked the grass. A blackbird killed a worm. A squirrel slipped off a slimy tree.

The back of my head hurt. My neck. Actually my whole body, right down to my feet. A meltdown. It started yesterday and has been gathering speed ever since.

It was Rina's fault. She said something really stupid yesterday and put me completely off track. I was just beginning to like her, and was hoping she wouldn't say something stupid – but then she did.

She said that she knew all about my problem. Her face widened with girlie concern.

'Like what?'

'Like I know you have this . . . disease.'

I just stared at her. 'Oh, yeah?'

'Sparrow told me it affects your skin. Something to do with your toes. And that you have to keep them always covered with special socks and that you have to go to a hospital now for treatment . . .'

'He's an idiot.'

'But I saw you going to the hospital this morning, from the bus.'

'Why do you listen to that birdbrain? He's an idiot.' I was getting angrier by her every word. Even *bus* made

115

me almost flip. I had been to see my father in hospital. It was a serious thing.

'I thought he's your friend.'

'*You* are an idiot.'

I shouldn't have said it. You can't call a girl an idiot and expect her to feel good about it.

[5]

I reckon we all actually live on separate planets, and that these planets seem to share the same space only to fool us. People see each other as if they are in the same place, but there is a glass bubble around each of us. We are like goldfish in separate bowls right next to each other. And the bowls are expandable. When you swim up against the edge, it moves out, so you never realize it is there. You swim and you swim and you swim, but you can never get there. Other people come close and gulp in your face, but you can't reach them. Gulp, gulp, gulp. Sink.

I didn't know what I really felt about Rina. Never mind her, I didn't even know what I felt about Sparrow. When I woke up this morning I realized Sparrow must have sneaked away my red socks after his rubbish about sole lines. But why? What kind of an animal would steal a pair of socks. Unwashed. Practically off my feet. A CD, I could understand. A mobile. Trainers, OK. But socks . . . is so, so unbelievably sad.

[6]

I heard the front door shut. My mother had learned to give up on goodbyes with me. I never answered. It was a point of principle. I learned it from my father.

The sudden emptiness of the house seemed to go straight to my stomach and drew me to the kitchen. I realized I did need sustenance.

When I entered, the refrigerator stopped humming as if it had sensed my presence. I opened it and stood in the glow of the milk light, waiting for the invisible intergalactic snowman inside to tell me the truth about myself. That what I needed was a sandwich. Ham, I heard it sigh. I wanted ham. Someone had tried to hide the ham by putting an economy-pack of low-fat yogurt on top. But no chance: five pink, vacuum-packed, honey-roasted slices peeped out, glistening with that green shine that suggests both a kind of greedy beauty and some exotic illness. I wanted ham in white bread – thick sliced – with loads of yellow butter. Nobody would see me make my sandwich, and nobody would see me eat it. Not my mother, not my father, not Lenny. The pleasure would be mine and mine alone.

I kicked the fridge door shut and put the packet on the table. A pile of sliced bread was leaning precariously against the toaster in an open polythene bag. In our house nobody seemed to close anything, except their minds. I took out two slices and placed them on a chopping board. They looked astonishing, like . . . well, just like two slices of white bread on a chopping board: flat, white, absorbent, patient, with brown edges that perfectly mirrored each other. I liked the way the edges looked a little warped on the top and curled out in a small lip at the corner.

I spread a huge blob of butter on one slice. Why is it yellow, if milk is so white? What is colour anyway? Light waves sinking and bouncing, the meaning entirely dependent on our eyes? If there were no eyes in the world, would there be colour? Would roses be red? And ham pink? Would pigment still be pigment, or would it be a state of pork? And my hand. What colour would it be, really?

I ran my thumb around the plastic shell of the packet of ham, feeling for the flap with which to peel the top off. When I found it, I pulled like tomorrow had definitely been postponed forever. No deal. I pulled again, and pulled the packet right out of my other hand. The ham stayed sealed. I grabbed a knife off the draining board and stabbed it. The packet went pop. The plastic flopped. I cut open the cover and teased out a couple of slices with the tip of the knife. They quivered a moment in the kitchen air before tumbling into the sink. 'Ham!' I cussed out aloud.

Sparrow's favourite cuss was pig head.

'Shouldn't it be pig-headed?' I asked him once, a little bookishly.

'Two syllables. Double punch.'

'What about fat face, then?'

'That's good too. But it's kind of literal. You have to think pig.' He laughed. 'Lateral. *Big.*'

I fished out the ham from the sink and slammed it on to the buttered bread. Slapped the other slice on top and stuffed it all in my mouth. *Ham.* That's the word I would go for. Ham you too, Sparrow. Damn sock thief.

[7]

Back on the sofa – belly filled – I figured the real trouble with Sparrow was that he didn't value friendship. He didn't care who his friends were. All he seemed to want was an audience. He liked to say things and he wanted someone to hear him; he liked to do things to provoke a reaction. It could be from anyone. It didn't seem to matter to him. Sparrow simply used people like they were lumps of clay. He seemed to want only to create an impression, to make a mark. Why? I couldn't understand this desire to have an effect on somebody, if that somebody could be anybody.

Sparrow was not the only one. Even my mother seemed to have this craving to make an impression on the anonymous. Dressing up, for example, whenever she stepped out of the house, like she was about to be whisked away to heaven. Or take chat-show clowns, or pop stars on TV, strutting about with their snouts twitching in the air, posing for people they would never ever know. People they couldn't even be sure existed. What was the point? At least with Sparrow there was some attachment to reality. At least he wanted some contact, even if he also wanted control. I didn't mind that. I could fight back. The problem was that Sparrow just didn't care *who* the other person was.

But despite that, there was something I liked about him. I guess it was because, unlike all those other people prancing about in the dark, on TV, or on the street, Sparrow was interested in something outside himself. From that, I felt, something meaningful could be made. I wanted to tell Sparrow about this possibility, but didn't know how to begin. It was all too vague. Just an idea that we could be on the verge of something new. A different kind of existence created out of astral DNA that would connect us all to one cosmic brain, which was the universe. I wanted to tell him that with a little bit of thinking we might work out that the time was now and that the waiting was over. That we already knew who we were and what we wanted. That we knew who our friends were. I imagined the sounds coming out of my mouth and falling apart, senselessly. 'What?' he'd spit with such contempt that I cringed even as I thought of it. It made me wish people could understand each other instantly. Wordlessly.

That is why I like the TV mute. The reason I don't usually say everything I want to.

Maybe I was already becoming like my father. He too used to hardly ever speak. He was always thinking – or seemed to be – but he didn't like to talk much. As though he thought that by putting it into words he might destroy the thing he was trying to describe.

Until, that is, yesterday at the hospital.

[8]

When we visited him yesterday Dad asked me to wait behind while the others went to find a vase for the flowers we'd brought. 'Listen, son, what keeps us apart sometimes is what keeps us together,' he said when we were alone.

'What do you mean?' I was mystified.

'You are young.'

'Yeah, Dad. Whatever.'

He rubbed at a bit of white stubble on his chin, filling the space between us with a deafening rasp. 'Listen, you need to understand that your mother is under a lot of strain. I guess we both have been.'

I stared at him as if I was seeing him for the first time in ages. He looked like a stranger in the ward. He was going bald on top and his skin had been sandpapered and smeared with ash. His eyes were bloodshot and there were heavy wrinkles like curtains gathered at the edges. Something had gone wrong with his whole shape. He had never looked like this before. He had always had neat black hair, sharp clean eyes and warm brown skin. His moustache was never lopsided. There had never been any grey in it. I could remember how I used to touch it to feel the thick, precise bristles. He used to be so much taller than me.

He coughed into his hand and cleared his throat. 'It hasn't been easy. I know I am not home much these days, but accounts are not like they used to be. I have to do the job the way they want me to, otherwise I'd lose everything.' He hesitated and glanced around the room. 'But your mother doesn't always appreciate how difficult it is, you know?'

I didn't know what there was to appreciate so much in the accounts department. His difficulties did not seem to be mine – yesterday. Silently, I studied the bunch of flowers lying on the bedside table. I didn't know what else to do. The waxy yellow paper was crumpled where she had clutched the stems. When I looked back at him, his eyes wobbled a little as though the blood in them was turning.

'You find out you can't always remember everything – where you started and where you are heading – when you are trying to keep everything balanced. Like on a tightrope, you know?'

'Tightrope?'

He gazed at me as if he was trying to focus down an unfamiliar road. 'You see, son, you discover life becomes a little bit like a . . .' He paused, as though he thought he ought to weigh the word in his mouth before letting it out again.

'What exactly are you trying to say?' I reckoned it was the drugs they must have given him. Serious clinical drugs.

His mouth opened again. I could see his lips were dry. There was a small blister at one corner and some thin, almost transparent, skin was peeling. I could hear air coming out of his mouth in small puffs. The panting became quieter as though some old-fashioned steam train was moving away from us into another world. He didn't say anything more for a while. Then he smiled weakly. 'Nothing. Nothing you don't already know, I guess, son.'

But all I knew was that the other day, while I was surfing off the sofa after school, he had suffered a severe chest pain and been rushed to hospital from his office. Apparently it was a mild heart attack. Nothing to worry about, I was told later, but he was going to be kept in hospital for a couple of days. OK. I had swallowed hard, pretending along with everyone else that it was not a real complaint. But, then, what was his body trying to say?

I could not understand how he had let himself go like that. Didn't he know how to take care of himself? Don't you learn that sort of thing as you grow older? That money isn't everything. That life isn't a circus. That you have to tend to things around you, look after yourself. That you can't just brood for years like a disgruntled foreigner and then, when you are bald and fat and tired, have a heart attack and start talking in ringside metaphors about life. My father was an accountant who had lost count, and yet he was now acting like some high-wire geezer in a collapsed tent.

Or was it me? Was I the one who was putting those words in his mouth?

Maybe it was really my mother's fault. Some sort of poetic justice for the way she sometimes, after one too many of her little Bell's, accused him of having no heart. He'd turn up the TV then and gulp down his own double Scotch, double fast. He'd watch any crap to escape a difficult conversation.

Maybe that was why she seemed so awkward with the flowers. Even so, I was glad when she came back down the ward with Lenny, carrying a big plastic jug full of hospital water.

[9]

The doorbell rang. I went to the front door and looked through the peephole.

'Oink, oink. Come on. Let's go. Rina's waiting at Blockbuster's.' Sparrow pressed the doorbell again, harder.

'OK, OK.' I unlocked the door. But did I want to see Rina ever again? What would I say now? What would she? And why was it that Sparrow was always there? I could see the three of us huddled together in front of a bunch of insane, overrated videos trying to agree on a film none of us really cared for. Would she be between Sparrow and me, or was I going to be the one in the middle? Or would it be Sparrow? Who was keeping whom apart? Was it the same one who was bringing us together?

I saw my father's grey face break into a fragile smile again.

'Come on.' Sparrow pulled my arm.

I shook him off. 'Wait, you've got my socks.'

'What?'

'You took them.'

'*Noh.*' Sparrow's voice went low, as though he was really saying, *What-you-have-lost-is-your-brain-dork.*

'What did you say to Rina about me?'

'You?'

'My feet.' I wanted to get a grip. I wanted my socks. I wanted more. Lots more.

Then I caught his eye and we both cracked up. I don't know why I laughed. I didn't care. For a brief moment, before my life changed from a trampoline to a tightrope, I didn't need words. Something miraculous rushed up my spine, linking each knot to the other, whistling and chortling and making me reel, freewheel, and feel every-thing was somehow going to be all right. That everything *was* all right. I was laughing. I couldn't stop laughing. It just burst out. I forgot all that had happened before. I forgot to worry about what might happen next. I forgot my father, my mother, my brother and me. I hopped on the thin bridge of the cold doorstep just laughing and laughing, and Sparrow laughed with me.

When we finally stopped, out of breath, he pulled a pair of red socks out of his back pocket and threw them in my face. 'Come on, hurry up. She's waiting for you, pig head.'

I slipped them on quickly, and then my trainers. My time had come. I knew it. I knew what to do. I'd see her, I'd go to the hospital. I'll do everything. I'll find a way – my own way – faster than my dad had ever even dreamed of.

In two minutes I was out, walking light on a rope stretched tight to infinity.

About the Wedding Feast

By Ama Ata Aido

(With a little warning for all those who may be allergic to the genre: that this is 'kitchen literature' with a vengeance – AAA)

It had began with the announcement itself. That those two were going to get married. My granddaughter just came in from her workplace one early evening and told us. No asking. It was all telling. That was when something hit me. Yes, from that early. That there was something not right already. In the old days, when things were done properly, a girl did not just announce that sort of thing in that sort of way. But later, when I pointed out to the child's mother, my daughter Mary, she said that things have changed.

. . . Hei, and how they have changed! . . . And of course, being my daughter Mary, hard as a palm kernel outside and coconut-soft inside, she later came and without apologising for speaking like that to me, asked me how the young lady should have informed us about what she and her young man intended . . .

And then there was the matter of the time. How can a serious discussion like marriage intentions start at the end of the day? In the old days, if a young woman wanted to bring up such a matter, she would begin by just hinting one of her mothers on her mother's side, who would hint her mother, who would then have hinted me her grandmother, and then I and her mother would have discreetly mentioned it to any other mothers and grandmothers whom we considered close enough to be brought into the discussions and the negotiations that would follow. Then, very early the next morning – at dawn really – we would have had a meeting, in my room certainly, sitting down properly, of course . . . But here I go again, forgetting that things have changed! In this case, the young lady came to just tell us. And that was how everything got handled. In the modern, educated way, and not at all properly.

Maybe, I should not have let myself grieve: since for a start, we were in a foreign land. The young man my granddaughter was going to marry is from one part of Africa that is quite far from our country. My daughter Mary had sent me a ticket to go and visit her and her husband and children. Indeed, let me tell the truth: when it comes to such gestures, Mary is good . . . so I had gone. As everybody knows, this was the second or third time. In fact, I was preparing to return home here when the announcement came from my grandchild. That was a blessing. Because, the way things have changed, I could sense that they were going to go ahead and finalise everything, when no one at home had the slightest knowledge about the proposed marriage. And then, what was I going to tell everybody when I came back? You would all have laughed at me, no? That I too had gone and lost my head abroad: the way all these educated people seem to do when they travel overseas.

So I said to Mary my daughter: 'Mary, it is true that things have changed, but have they really changed that much?'

'Maybe not, Mother . . . you only worry too much,' was what she said. Now tell me, what kind of a response was that?

Anyway, that was when I came back here and informed you all about it. I had been quite surprised and very relieved that you had all been so understanding. Was it you or Abanowa who had suggested that since the child was in a foreign land anyway, and the young man she was marrying does not come from anywhere around here, everybody should accept that there was no question of anybody getting the chance to go and check his background to make sure everything about him and his family was satisfactory, and so if I found him acceptable, that should be fine with you all? At the time, I had not commented on it, but oh, I was so grateful for that.

As I had informed you all at the family meeting, I knew Mary was going to be sending me a ticket to go back there for the wedding. But she had sent it much earlier . . . Mary doesn't know how to do a lot of things. In that she is not alone. It's the education. It takes away some very important part of understanding from them . . . But then, I must also say for Mary that those things she knows how to do, she does them very well.

So, that was how I came to be present at the big meeting between Mary and the boy's mother about what should be prepared for the wedding feast . . . To tell the truth, I had not really felt too happy at the idea of a joint discussion. It was not right. What self-respecting family in the old days would ask for help from their prospective in-laws? Whether it was in the way of just ideas or for something more substantial like the actual preparation of the food for the wedding feast? But when I so much as opened my mouth, Mary said that these days, that is not only all right, but even expected. She added that in fact, she might hurt feelings if she didn't ask for the help. Mmm, things have really changed, haven't they?

Since there was not going to be any grandmother from the boy's side at the meeting, Mary and I agreed that I would sit in on the discussions, but would keep a respectable silence. Which is what I did. However, every now and then, my daughter whispered questions to me to which I gave discreet answers.

It had not seemed as if there was much disagreement about anything. They had discussed everything in a friendly way: the wedding cake itself; other cakes; biscuits and buns; how to do the peanuts and the other things for the guests to munch and crunch . . .

Peanuts? O yes, they are everywhere! . . .

They had sat and talked for a long time, may be for as much as half the day, when they came to the foods that called for real cooking. That was when things began to take time to decide. I had been thinking, and even told them, that if they did not stop for a little rest and get something to eat, something nasty was going to happen. But Mary said, and it was plain the boy's mother agreed with her, that it was better to finish everything at a sitting. I was going to open my mouth and tell them that since the beginning of creation, no family had finished planning what should go into a wedding feast at one sitting. But then I remembered that things had changed, and warned my lips.

Then it happened and I was not at all surprised. I had heard Mary mention jolof and other dishes from our country. Then maybe, for just the shortest bit of time, I had got lost in my own thoughts and had not paid attention to the discussions. Because I had not noticed that something had come up which was really cutting their tempers short. All I saw was suddenly, Mary and the boy's mother standing up at the same time and each of them shouting:

'That's no food and you are not serving it at my daughter's wedding.'

'That's no food and you are not serving it at my son's wedding.'

'Spinach stewed with a mixture of meat and fish?' shouted one with a sneer that was big enough to wither a virgin forest.

'Spinach stewed with only onions and without meat or fish?' shouted the other, the contempt in her voice heavy enough to crush a giant.

'What do you mean?' shouted one.

'What do you mean?' countered the other.

'I said that's no food, and you are not going to serve it at my child's wedding!' they both screamed at the same time.

'You cannot tell me that,' one wailed.

'You cannot tell me that,' the other whined after her.

'Our guests will not eat that,' one spat out.

'Our guests will laugh at us if you serve that,' said the other.

'They will tell everyone in our community.'

'They will write home to everyone in our country about it.'

'It is awful, a mess.'

'Yours is unclean.'

'Yours is completely tasteless.'

'But you ate it when you came to our house!' said one, perplexed.

'But you ate it when you came to our house!' said the other, equally perplexed.

'No, I didn't. I didn't touch it,' they both confessed.
'Eh?!'
'I went and threw it into the rubbish bin in the kitchen.'
'W–h–a–t?'
They made as if they were going to clutch at each other's throats.
'Mother, Mother, what is this?'
None of us who were already in the room had seen or felt my granddaughter and the young man come in. But they had.
'What is this?' they repeated. The mothers stopped dead. Shame on their faces, each stared at the girl and the boy in the hallway. For what seemed to be a very long time, there was complete silence. Then the boy and the girl looked at one another, burst out laughing, didn't stay to say anything else to anybody and then went out of the room, still laughing.
What did the mothers do? What could they do? Each of them just sat down and stayed sat. And quiet. After some time, I called my daughter Mary's name.
'What is it?' she asked, glaring at me.
'Listen,' I said, my voice low. 'I think you people had better stop now and continue with the planning of the feast tomorrow.'
'What is there to plan? . . . Anyway, I am finished with all that,' Mary said. And with that she went out of the room.
And that's how everything ended with the food affair. O yes, there was a wedding. And it was not only the ceremony itself that went well. Everything else was wonderful. We cooked our palaver sauce of spinach with egusi, meat and fish. The boy's people cooked their very

plain spinach, without meat or fish . . . And did the guests eat? Don't even ask. They ate and ate and ate and ate. Since then, I have not heard that anyone from the boy's side complained about the food we cooked. And I am not hearing anyone from our side complain about the food our in-laws cooked . . .

You see o . . . what still puzzles me is how people can tell others how much things have changed, when they do not prepare their own minds to handle such changes, eh?! . . . And as my mother used to say: 'What is food anyway? Once it goes down the throat . . .'

The Publishers would like to thank the following for permission to reproduce copyright material:

Acknowledgements

AMA ATA AIDOO: 'About the Wedding Feast' from *The Girl Who Can and Other Stories* (Heinemann African Writer's Series, 2000). Reprinted by permission of Harcourt Education; MEI CHI CHAN: 'Snowdrop' from *Dim Sum: British Chinese Short Stories* (Crocus Books, 1997); SAMUEL FEIJOO: 'Private Eloy' from *Cuba: An Anthology for Young People* (Young World Books, 1983); ROMESH GUNESEKARA: copyright © Romesh Gunesekara. Reprinted by permission of A. M. Heath & Co. Ltd. Authors' Agents.'Tightrope' from *Walking a Tightrope: New Writing from Asian Britain*, edited by Rehana Ahmed (Macmillan Children's Books, 2004); EVAN HUNTER: 'On the Sidewalk Bleeding', originally published in Manhunt (1957), recently published in collection *Barking at Butterflies and Other Stories* (Thorndike Five-Star, 2000), copyright © 1957,